To: Chronicle/Examiner
For your reference library, please accept
this book.
Happy reading. Enjoy!
Humbly, Virgie V. Jones

Be It Ever So Humble...

Be It Ever So Humble ...

A pictorial, social history
with personalized footnotes

by

Virgie V. Jones

Morris-Burt Press, Alamo, California, 1983

Published By
MORRIS-BURT PRESS
10 Gary Way
Alamo, California 94507

Printed in the United States of America
Pioneer Publishing Company, Fresno, California

In Memory of

My late husband, Alfred Bensen Jones, who because of his known heritage, as a native of Alamo, introduced me to the San Ramon Valley, and our home we built together in Alamo in 1948. May he rest in peace.

Table of Contents

Author's Foreword

It's been several years since the November 1977 release of my last book, *Historical Persons and Places... in San Ramon Valley*. And though I used the identical sign-off in its epilogue, May 1977, I did not intend it as any promise of another book on the San Ramon Valley area.

However, you, my readers, think otherwise, and I have received questions on when I'd be doing another book on this area.* And so the embryonic stage of this book was begun April 30, 1983, which was five years and five months since the last one was released for your perusal. This author has not had her head in the sand in that time. Several accomplishments and several trips* have been realized. A new medium in creative writing was born.

Because it has been difficult for me to understand much of the contemporary poetry being published currently, I decided to take a turn at some, for my own amusement. My first attempt was short and sweet, and perhaps has become my favorite. It was published May 1980 in "California in Rhyme and Rhythm I," compiled by the Conference of California Historical Societies, Stockton. I'll share it with you:

HAPPINESS

Happiness is...
Good Health—
Some wealth—
and Love.

Appearing in the same publication was a second attempt which I entitled "Springtime." It was twice as long with two stanzas. And during that period of my poetry endeavors, some dozen or more developed. Some can be found in poetry anthologies published by The World of Poetry Press, Sacramento, edited by Eddie-Lou Cole. In July 1981, my "Rainbow" appeared in "The World's Great Contemporary Poems." In April 1982, "A Meadow" was printed in "The Family Treasury of Great Poems," and later in 1982 a poem I called "Cats" appeared in "Our Twentieth Century's Greatest Poems." Another was accepted for publication in 1983, though I decined the offer. It has become another favorite of mine, and I call it "Birthdays—Who Needs Them?" It received an award in the category of creative writing at the Federated Women's District Convention at Stockton in mid-April 1983. I shall continue my contemporary poetry creations, as they are fun to do, especially for my own amusement and self-criticism. As one of my poems says, modern poetry and ultra-contemporary poetry need not have rhythm or meter and are often words on paper. Oh, lest I forget—along the way there were also several rejection slips! And, when necessary, I continue my letters-to-the-editors*—regarding my opinions on community problems.

The "straw that broke this author's back" must have been the unnecessary removal of the last Italian cypress tree at Danville Boulevard and Stone Valley Road, to spur me on to do this book.

We know the cypress is an evergreen tree, member of the pine family and native of North America, Europe and Asia. It is very hardy in California and the Gulf states. there are twelve, some references say fifteen, species—many varieties distinctive in form which can attain eighty feet, and some that will go as high as one hundred fifty feet. The tree is ornamental and picturesque in maturity. Age gives them all a singular beauty that lends itself to a garden of simple design. Like other long-lived trees, the cypress should be given more consideration in garden design. It is propagated by seed or cuttings.

It is presumed that the stand of six Italian cypress trees were planted when the first Alamo

Grammar School was built there in 1876, maybe by the pupils. Mary Ann (Smith) Jones sold the two and a quarter acres for school use only, for $200. Or these trees could have been on the Jones property for many years and been planted by the early Spanish settlers. We must believe that these trees were at least 107 years old. Longtimers I've interviewed have always remembered these trees being near all three of the grammar schools on this site. They cannot be replaced.

Why dwell on it now? Hopefully to safeguard against this action ever happening again! Right next door to the south we can see an excellent example of good planning. Again commendation goes to Jeanne Ader, owner of Jeanne's Fashions, and her late husband Roy, the builder, and to Jean Johnston of San Ramon, interior designer, for the beautiful job they did when they developed the former Cross property, purchased from the daughter Alma (Cross) Crosby, of New York and Jamaica, by Al and Mary Madison September 13, 1974. After Al died, Mary sold it to the Aders, in 1979. All the lovely redwood trees were respected and remain. The planning was done to accommodate these trees. December 1979 was the opening of the beautiful Les Boutiques d'Alamo, which in addition to Jeanne's Fashions includes six rentals. It is always a pleasure to visit this well-planned group of shops and the attractive courtyard.

Developers can do better—if they and their architects only try. I'm so tired of the "plastic look" of new buildings.

I'm proud to say I serve on the newly organized Tree Ordinance Committee which met with Supervisor Robert Schroder for the first time June 23, 1983, following the plans neighboring Walnut Creek and Lafayette use.

Actually—if you know me—you know I wear my heart on my sleeve. I'm born under the ninth zodiacal sign of Sagittarius with Jupiter rising. As they say, "If Jupiter is with you, nobody can be against you!" I'm proud of my sign, even though the directness of this sign can lead to having one's foot in the mouth on occasion. And telling it like it is is not always received as offered. But it's challenging—and I love a challenge!

History is not like "new math." We researchers strive for accuracy. But using the sub-title "social history" gives us some leeway!

Author's footnotes: Maybe if I fantasize, I would hope to be doing a racy, sexy historical novel, and make my fame and fortune. But I can't write that way, and I can't seem to get out of the San Ramon Valley area too far in my writings.

Trips—Enjoyed seeing several other parts of our world. In 1979, with my husband, enjoyed our last trip together by returning to the Hawaiian Islands. In 1981, with my longtime girlfriend from first grade days, did Greece and Turkey with a cruise, visiting several of their islands. In 1982, with another friend, took a first trip to the British Isles and found the natives to be friendly and warm people. In 1983, with another friend and former Alamoite, had a first peek at the Orient with all its wonders and aged mysteries. In 1984 back to Europe for the fourth time to witness the 350th year celebration of the "Passion Play" at Oberammergau and finally to Italy. These, plus short trips to Reno, Yosemite Valley, Southern California, and an initial visit to the fabulous Hearst Castle and Carmel/Monterey, have broadened my horizon.

It has been suggested that my next book be copies of my letters-to-the-editors. Who knows? Only time will tell!

Acknowledgements and Credits

California's Spanish Place-Names, What They Mean and How They Got There, by Barbara and Rudy Marinacci. Presidio Press, San Rafael, CA, 1980.

Preliminary Historic Resources Inventory. Contra Costa County, CA, 1976.

John Muir 1838-1914: John of the Mountains, by Linnie Marsh Wolfe.

La Fayette: A Pictorial History, by Sandy Kimball. Lafayette Historical Society, 1976.

Some California Poppies & Even a Few Mommies, Vol. 1, by Dorothy Gittinger Mutnick. 1980.

The History of Orinda, Gateway to Contra Costa County, by Muir Sorrick. Orinda Library Board, Inc., Friends of the Orinda Library, Orinda, CA. 1970.

Historical Sketches Recalling Early Times and People of the Pinole, California Area, by Jessie Howe Clark. 1979.

This Point in Time. The Point Richmond History Association. 1980.

Benicia: Portrait of an Early California Town, by Robert Bruegmann. 101 Productions, San Francisco. 1980.

In Old Diablo, by Arnold Blackmur. Ampex Corporation, Redwood City, CA. 1981.

The World Book Encyclopedia. Field Enterprises Educational Corp., Chicago, Ill. 1958.

The New Garden Encyclopedia. Wm. H. Wise and Co., New York. 1945.

San Ramon Valley Old Timer (newspaper). May 1, 1939, Vol. 1, No. 1, published for Pioneer Celebration, Danville, CA.

Oakland Tribune, Sunday Supplement. Oakland, CA. February 26, 1961.

Contra Costa Times, a division of Lesher Communications, Inc., Walnut Creek, CA.

Tri-Valley News. Floyd Sparks, Bay Area Publishing Co., Inc., Hayward, CA.

San Ramon Valley Herald. Floyd Sparks, Bay Area Publishing Co., Inc., Hayward, CA.

Valley Pioneer, a division of Lesher Communications, Inc., Danville, CA.

California Highways and Public Works, May-June 1965.

In all modesty I must list my own two books, as they were good sources for material used: *Remembering Alamo . . . and Other Things Along the Way*, 1975, and *Historical Persons and Places . . . in San Ramon Valley*, Vol. 2, 1977, both Morris-Burt Press, Alamo, CA.

Special appreciation and thanks to those people whom I contacted in personal interviews, by telephone or correspondence, who shared their knowledge with me so I could share it with my readers, and to those who supplied photographs, which will be donated to the San Ramon Valley Historical Society photo files. Also to the readers of my first two books who spurred me on to get to writing another book. This I chose to do on old buildings and homes built before 1920, before they will be in memory only.

Endorsed by: the San Ramon Chamber of Commerce, San Ramon Valley Historical Society, Contra Costa County Board of Supervisors, and San Ramon City Council.

Prologue

When I was a paid by-lined newspaper columnist, I once had an editor who would often say, "Virgie, stop editorializing!" And I'd respond, "I'm not—I'm philosophizing." And I was—and I like to feel I still do.

There are those that think we authors are making our fortunes writing. A two-year study made by Columbia University and released by Associated Press showed that American authors make less than $5,000 a year on the average from writing. And, by the hour, writing books pays no better than being a file clerk or a janitor. It also found that men make more than women in writing, and not surprisingly, writers of racy books do better than poets!

One out of five authors of romance, detective, western or Gothic books may hit a $50,000 level of income. Among those making less than $2,500, 55 percent write poetry or academic non-fiction, the study further showed. Thirty-eight percent of authors teach at colleges and universities and 20 percent are professionals, i.e. doctors, lawyers, or among the clergy. Another interesting statistic was that among married female authors, the median income of husbands was $26,000, while for wives of writing husbands it was under $4,000.

These figures were compiled for the Authors Guild Foundation by Columbia's Center for Social Sciences, based on responses from 2,239 authors about their incomes in 1979. An author was defined as a writer who had at least one book published. None surveyed hit million-dollar movie, paperback sales in 1979, but a small percentage that participated in the survey had books that made the best seller list and accounted for the few six-figure incomes of 1979. The top 10 percent of all authors surveyed were in the $45,000-plus range and the top 5 percent had writing incomes of $80,000 or better.

Nearly half the authors put in twenty-five hours at the typewriter per week even if they held other occupations. Twelve percent of these writers worked less than ten hours per week at writing. If paid by the hour, the median rate for all the authors would be $4.90, compared to a file clerk's earnings of $4.95 plus job benefits, or a janitor's at $4.49. The current federal minimum wage is $3.35 per hour and a typical factory hand in metropolitan New York makes $7.35.

So you say, okay—so why write? Good question. My answer, and I can only answer for myself, is because we enjoy it—and we feel we have a message to share. And now that you know I'm not making my fame or fortune writing these California regional history books, I hope you can appreciate the time and effort it takes. When one is not gainfully employed, time is free. Effort is another thing—and energy is a big factor too. I thank the good Lord, fortunately I have both—and I'll admit it—I'm tenacious! (A handwriting expert told me that once years ago.)

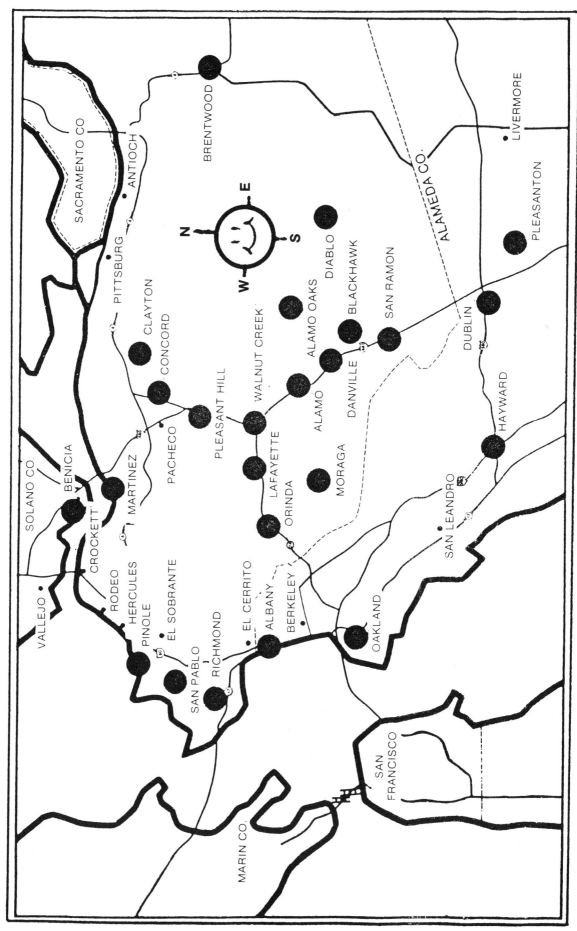

Chapter One

Roads and Progress

On May 17, 1852, the establishment of the county road, north to south, from Martinez to San Jose, was recorded in Volume 1 of the Record of the Court of Sessions, page 78. Ten years later, the county was taking title to lands throughout the valley, to establish a public roadway of greater traffic capacity. On March 8, 1862, Daniel and Andrew Inman, August Hemme, Erastus Ford, and others, deeded a portion of their lands to the public use. The property owners who deeded land to the county did not go unpaid. The standard rate was one dollar per landowner, regardless of the length of the strip across his property!

The legal description of the property begins: "Commencing at a stake standing nearly in front of the Blacksmith shop of Joseph Flippen in the town of Danville; thence running in the general direction of the creek called San Ramon to another stake standing—in front of the barn belonging to H. W. Harris; thence to another stake—a little north—; thence to about 19 steps from an oak tree standing on the bank of the creek marked with a blaze on the westside . . . " The county may have been vague in its land description but it was definite that a sixty-foot wide strip was required.

In May of 1862 a like strip was procured running from the corner of the A. W. Hammett house, across the bridge and up to the gate near the house of Orris Fales. This was the most northerly action of the road through the valley, since Fales' home can be found on old maps to be located near Walnut Creek (what some call South Walnut Creek).

While the north to south roadway was being established, cross paths were developing. In 1858, one was known only as "the road from Alamo to Wilson Coats' home in Green Valley." This was named Kent Road in 1892, and we now know it as Green Valley Road. County records first note

Norris Canyon Road in 1865, with a portion called Stanley Road, and Crow Canyon appears in 1867.

On an old map dated 1871 were shown five main thoroughfares through the valley. These were the north to south roadway, called "road to San Jose," Crow Canyon, Stone Valley, Tassajara and Diablo roads. Tassajara had several names, one being Carneal Road, until it officially became Camino Tassajara in 1892.

Added to these five roads in 1885 were Norris Canyon and Livorna and the southern stretch of Bollinger Canyon Road had been laid. It reached to a point almost directly west of Danville and ended at the corner of the Lawrence and Pierce properties.

Southern Pacific Railway built its San Ramon branch and by 1891 the train ran to Danville. A map of 1894 shows the track ran only to the townsite of San Ramon, but an extension had been proposed to reach the county line. Three stations were spotted along the valley. Hemme Station* served Alamo and was located between the creek and the road, almost where Hemme Avenue meets the highway today. Danville Station was on the southeast edge of town, the village being mainly between the railroad and the creek. The San Ramon Station was on the north boundary of the Norris section of Rancho San Ramon and access was by Fostoria Way.

With the coming of the railroad, the valley opened up for the first surge of population growth. Comparisons of two old maps, ten years apart in drawing, show the expansion. "City" streets grew rapidly more numerous; Front Street in Danville was widened to carry the traffic, and many private roads sprang up. Each ranch had its own access road, generally bearing the family name— Kuss, Hartz, Love, Meese, Baldwin, Stone and Reis, to name a few.

It is interesting to note that, with the exception of Tassajara, most of the older roads bore "eastern-type" or family names. It was not until the turn of the century that the Spanish influence was again felt strongly.

Research turns up other branch lines* in railroading to be: Avon, Galindo, Nacio, Hookston, Las Juntas, Walnut Creek, Alamo, Hemme, Danville, Osage, San Ramon and Forest Home.

INTERSTATE ROUTE 680

Gold discovery of January 24, 1848 at Coloma, California on the American River near Sacramento brought a population of 10,000 to that small community. It opened up migration to the west and California in particular.

So too, in 1965, when Freeway 680 opened up parts of Contra Costa County to home dwellers. And the building and development and subdivisions of former ranch properties came to the San Ramon Valley. Though it had begun in the late 1940s to some degree, the coming of the freeway really set off a continual migration from the Bay Area cities and elsewhere.

Many servicemen from other states who served in California camps, upon discharge remembered the green and gold of the California hillside countryside and brought their brides and families out "to live in the country." Many who had come to work in the shipyards never returned to their native states or former homes. Industries and companies came later and continue to arrive and have settled in the San Ramon Valley, especially in the new city of San Ramon.

A notable change from "country" to bedroom community came in 1965, when construction was completed on 6.7 miles of four-lane freeway on Interstate 680 between Danville and Walnut Creek. This project had been open to traffic and Interstate 680 had functioned as a full freeway from Danville to the Benicia-Martinez Bridge since early December 1964. The Danville to Walnut Creek contract was the largest single roadway contract let to date in the bay area and required almost three years to complete, at a cost of $13,750,000. Separation structures for interchanges and local traffic provided for Sycamore Valley, Diablo, El Pintado, El Alamo, El Monte, Stone Valley, Rudgear and Livorna roads. Four bridges were constructed over San Ramon Creek and overheads were built over the Southern Pacific Railroad at Danville and at South Walnut Creek.

DOUBLE D—
DANVILLE-DUBLIN FREEWAY

February 4, 1965, construction began on the Danville-Dublin link. This final link in Contra Costa County followed the historic corridor which first was a stagecoach route, then state highway 21 and since 1966 an interstate freeway. It now provides a modern, safer facility to the rapidly growing San Ramon Valley. It made it possible for motorists to completely circle the entire East Bay area, a seventy-three-mile loop, without having to stop for one traffic signal! This well-planned freeway network took additional traffic loads off city streets and conventional highways. And of course it brought the growth and development to the communities.

The route was first adopted September 1957 at a cost of $5,411,887 for the 5.9 miles. Access to the freeway was provided at Crow Canyon Road* and bridges were constructed across San Ramon Creek. Other structures include undercrossings at Pine Valley Road and Donegal Avenue and overcrossings at Bollinger Canyon and Norris Canyon roads and County Road "D" (North San Ramon) to provide local traffic separation. The cost of right of way was $4,430,000. This is in contrast to the two dollars per acre that James Witt Dougherty paid to Jose Maria Amador for 10,000 acres in 1849.

Interstate 680 between Route 580 and one mile north of the Alameda-Contra Costa line slightly over three miles of freeway was constructed. Interchange facilities at the intersection of routes 580 and 680 and at Alcosta Boulevard and separation structures at Amador Valley and Dublin boulevards.

As a part of the project, Interstate 580 was widened from four to eight lanes within the limits of the Route 580/680 interchange. Frontage roads were constructed on Alcosta Boulevard, and bridges over the Alamo Canal. $5,312,000 was allotted for the work with a joint venture of Green Construction Company and Winston Brothers Company.

Project facts: Length and Limits: 5.9 miles from 0.6 miles north of Alameda-Contra Costa county line to 0.3 miles south of Sycamore Valley Road near Danville. Construction started February 4, 1965. Contractor was Fredrickson and Watson. Project superintendent was Clarence Buck. Con-

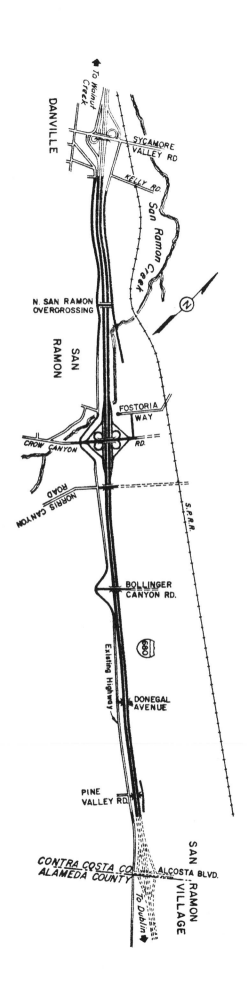

struction engineer was J. F. O'Brien and resident engineer was George Nakagawa.

The dedication ceremonies* were held September 24, 1966, commencing at 11:00 A.M. This Double D—Danville to Dublin Freeway Celebration was sponsored by the San Ramon Valley Chamber of Commerce, with Dr. Wilson E. Close its chairman. Committee members who assisted him were: Alfred Jones, Virginia Deaton, James Graham, Walt Lucas, Ted Merrill, Semmes Gordon, Keith Harris, Al Kaplan, Bill McGregor and Bud Spencer. A reception and luncheon for dignitaries and community-spirited participants was held in the Danville Hotel's Silver Dollar banquet room.

*Author's footnotes:

Hemme Station—I remember the sign well. It stayed there for many years after the trains no longer ran. I also remember seeing several of the others named.

Branch lines—How many can you position on today's maps?

Crow Canyon. It is not known for sure whether Crow Canyon was named for the Krough family in the vicinity or the crows that flew over the area.

Dedication Ceremonies. I was asked to be a hostess for the day and I still have my hostess badge and credentials.

My thanks to Norman F. Root, secretary, Historic Preservation Committee of the Department of Transportation, Division of Highways and Programming at Sacramento, for some of this informaiton and the following historical anecdote: Mr. Root was the bridge resident engineer on the Interstate 680 Danville to Walnut Creek Project, in March 1965. A group planned an opening celebration to be held at the Stone Valley Road Interchange in Alamo. One of the state surveyors, employed on the project, was a sky diving hobbyist. He made arrangements for the committee to pay for an airplane ride for himself and three friends. They were to parachute into one of the interchange loops at the high point of the ceremony. The airplane got off course due to unaccounted for wind that day. The divers could not even see the target as they jumped, but thought they would be able to maneuver their chutes in flight so as to land on target at the appropriate moment. The newspaper account the following day described a group of red-faced sky divers who were embarrassed by landing in various backyards some miles away from the ceremony site! (I remember the incident well—I was there.)

On Thursday, July 28, 1983, Caltrans workers installed signs designating Interstate 680 and Highway 24 in Contra Costa and Alameda counties as "Scenic Highways." The highway follows the route of nineteenth century stagecoach lines. Highway 24 was voted into

3

existence in 1931 and became a four-lane road between Walnut Creek and the Caldecott Tunnel in 1943. The interchange of the two highways was completed in 1965. State and county officials attended a ceremony July 28, 1983, commemorating the designation.

MOCKINGBIRDS

Mockingbirds—
Like roosters—
Have no sense of time.
Their copying of songs
   Anytime—
    All day—and
Somtimes half the night!

APPLES

Apples—I love apples!
Apples—are rosy red or
Apples—are sunny yellow or
Apples—are green in color
    but ripe for use
Apples—are yummy raw
   but super in applesauce, apple juice
   and of course Mom's apple pies
For years it's been said
   "An apple a day—keeps the doctor away"
And—maybe they do
   The pectin gives us energy
But woe—look what the apple did to
   Adam—and his Eve—
   In their garden—at Eden.

Chapter Two

Changes

Since the release of my *Historical Persons and Places...In San Ramon Valley* in November of 1977, many changes have taken place in the San Ramon Valley of Contra Costa County in northern California. Of course the rapid growth we all expected would come, did, and it continues at a rapid rate. The greatest—has been more people which always means more facilities and services for their needs. And, incorporation once again was on the agenda—to do, or not to do—and all the controversies it brings.

With the election of June 8, 1982, the 124-year-old town of Danville legally became a city, though its mayor and council prefer it be called a "town." Election returns showed 5,725 yes, with 4,850 no. On July 1, 1982, its first city council was sworn in and were: John May, Beverly Lane, Dick McNeely, Susanna Schlendorf and Doug Offenhartz, and local merchant John May became mayor.

To the south, neighboring San Ramon, voraciously developing and growing, also incorporated at a special election held March 8, 1983. Outcome was 3,825 yes and 1,254 no. City council members are: Diane Schinnerer, Richard Harmon, Mary Lou Oliver, Wayne Bennett and Jerry Ajlouny, and they prefer to be called a city. Its city government has a woman at the helm with Diane Schinnerer sworn in as of July 1983. Both cities altered their territorial boundaries.

Alamo, the oldest town in the San Ramon Valley, with an established post office by May 18, 1852, still remains unincorporated, even though it was the first to consider such a move way back in 1956. Feasibility studies are being considered for the benefit of this town's future destiny.

And, the "orphan" of the San Ramon Valley, Diablo, remains to itself and never wanted any part of it all, and probably never will!—and plays its role low-key.

With these changes will come many more changes. With all the expansion will come continued development and construction—and people—bodies. Since the area still has several old buildings intact—it is questionable how long they will be allowed to remain. It is with this thought, of their possible removal or destruction, that it became necessary for me to once again record on paper some of them for posterity.

As I've mentioned before, there is no way that this book can contain all the historical homes and buildings. And, there are other old homes, here and there, that I may not be aware of and others with such sketchy backgrounds of research that they would not make good reading. As you read, you will note several of these buildings researched are no longer on their original site. Buildings were often moved elsewhere—and that practice has continued.

Herein, the attempt has been to give you homes most acceptable and those still in use and all built before 1920. And, isn't it nice to learn there are still as many here to share with you in this *Be It Ever So Humble . . .*

SAN RAMON CHAMBER OF COMMERCE

Sixty years after the Greater San Ramon Valley Chamber of Commerce developed out of the San Ramon Valley Improvement Club, April 25, 1923, a splinter group left its nest! The San Ramon area, following its incorporation, decided to venture alone. A group of San Ramon merchants found the need to form their own group to accommodate the current 740 businesses. An organizational get-together was April 1983, and the San Ramon Chamber of Commerce was born. In a one-month period there were 150 members. Memberships are in six categories and dues run from $50 to $175 per year.

Two-year members of the board of directors elected were: John T. Dockery, Larry La Grandeur, Dean Auch, Jack Wood, Judy Macfarlane and Monte Adams. One-year members were: Pam Arthur, Dick Robello, Pat Brocker, Don Thiele, Delores Tuohy. Alternates were: Pat Hampton, Terri Possin, Vic Moreno and Phil White.

On June 24, 1983, at the first meeting of the board of directors, the following officers were elected: John T. Dockery, president; Pam Arthur, vice-president; Larry La Grandeur, treasurer; and Delores Tuohy, secretary.

Active committees are: membership, finance, communications, planning, economic development, community affairs, government liaison. A monthly newsletter called "San Ramon Chamber View" is published with a calendar of events, membership update, a profile of a chamber member, president's message, and some paid advertisements. The photographer is John Komperda. In July 1983 the president's message read in part: "This chamber has the desire to integrate the businesses, residential, educational, and political aspects of the San Ramon community in helping formulate growth to the new city."

There is a Monthly Membership Mixer (3M), a social gathering the last Tuesday of the month. Temporary offices are at 3211 Crow Canyon Place, Suite A-80, San Ramon. The installation dinner was August 28, 1983 at the San Ramon National Golf and Country Club on Fircrest Lane. It was "San Ramon Chamber Day."

Chapter Three

Statistics

One big problem in determining the ages of homes or buildings is the "stretching of time"! If it is rumored to be old, someone is always willing to tack on additional years to make it older—often how "antiques" are born. Wouldn't it be helpful if old buildings could talk? The stories they could tell! In my research, over the years, it has been interesting to work with progressions of ownerships to learn the diversity buildings have experienced. Chains of title often leave a lot to be desired, but they are legal and if it's not recorded in the county books, it's not legal. How well I know!

Houses, like people, acquire names, and through the years very often those names stick and we refer to buildings and houses by the names that applied years ago when certain occupants lived there for long periods. They seemed to leave their mark. Sometimes they were not necessarily ever owners.

The San Ramon Valley, which includes the towns and cities of Alamo*, Danville*, Diablo and San Ramon*, according to the last census of 1980, has a population of 56,820. It covers some seventy-two square miles. This lovely valley is nestled and in the protection of majestic Mount Diablo with its 3,849-foot elevation. The valley also includes Blackhawk and Tassajara*.

The San Ramon Valley is in Contra Costa County with its population of 650,155, in northern California. Elevation is 125 to 360 feet. The climate enjoys a long period of summer weather for much outdoor living with annual sunny days 290 to 310 days. Average minimum temperature is 51.3 degrees Fahrenheit, maximum 72.9, with a mean temperature of 59.8 degrees Fahrenheit. The highest recorded is 114 degrees and the lowest is 17. Average rainfall is 21 inches.

The 1982-83 winter-into-spring seasons broke rain records for most of northern California. The San Ramon Valley was no exception! News releases wrote of 200-year records being broken. Though no one was keeping weather records in 1783. However, whenever average seasonal rainfall doubles, meteorologists label it a 200-year occurrence. Dr. Paul Wu, Contra Costa County meteorologist, reports that, according to his statistics, the 200-year rainfall has been exceeded in Danville and in the Oakley-Antioch areas. In Danville the average rainfall is 22.4 inches, but by April 30, 1983, it had reached 47.01 inches.

Mount Diablo, on the average, receives 21.4 inches a year. But by the end of April 1983, 42.21 inches had fallen. In the county, Orinda holds the title for being the wettest, beating out neighboring Moraga by two inches. At Saint Mary's College there had been 54.2 inches in that same time period. At the East Bay Municipal Utility filter plant in Orinda 56.5 inches were recorded. Dr. Wu claims, "There is no 'normal' rain year—talk is about averages. Every year is different."

The unusual part was to have an exceptionally wet 1981-82 followed by another record-breaking year, 1982-83—back-to-back. Long-time east county farmers can't remember a worse year, with frequent rains falling at the wrong times. Deputy Agricultural Commissioner Ed Meyer said, "Every time the ground seemed almost dry enough to get into the fields to prepare for planting, the rains returned."

The rain hasn't been all bad! Range lands are verdant and cattle will be well-fed. The snow-pack in the Sierra hit records also, bringing threats of Delta flooding when it melts. However, it will mean better water for Contra Costa residents.

And now, back to the San Ramon Valley's historical buildings. It wasn't too difficult to select the buildings to use in this book. Several I have used over the years, in the tours I devised for groups, e.g. cubs, boy and girl scouts, 4-H groups, garden clubs, etc. Regardless of what you've heard, there is *no* "historical walking tour" as such of any consequence in the San Ramon Valley. The area is spread out too much for that. The one I suggest is recommended via bicycle or motorcade. For safety and convenience, all the buildings on the tour are on the west side of San Ramon Valley Boulevard—the Las Trampas range side.

As in many other areas, many homes in the San Ramon Valley had their beginnings as little more than cabins. Lots of them had their start as summer homes only, primarily because of the long summer season. Owners who lived in other Bay Area cities would invest in property in the San Ramon Valley and build dwellings to meet those needs. As years passed by, these same homes were improved with modern facilities added, like heating systems, improvements of kitchens and bathrooms, and of course, additions and modernizing. And the updating continues—and the appreciation is realized.

But the "Grande Dames"—the Victorian types—built in the mid and late 1800s, were erected on a larger floor plan and more permanent. They, too, had facelifts when needed. Among them we are lucky to have those recommended for this tour: Podva House, A. J. Young Home, Spilker House, "El Nido"—Harlan Rancho, David Glass Home, "Forest Home Farms"—Boone Home.

Author's footnotes: According to the 1980 census: Alamo, 8,410; Danville, 26,181; San Ramon, 22,229.

Blackhawk and Tassajara currently are part of geographic Danville, but developing at a rapid rate and may someday wish to be on their own with their own zip code number.

Danville population 27,880 according to the new sign erected at the southerly border, north of Crow Canyon Road, July 9, 1983.

Mount Diablo—On Saturday, August 20, 1983, Mount Diablo was designated as a National Natural Landmark by the Department of the Interior. It is among thirty-one California sites and one of two in the Bay Area. The other is in Marin County. There was a ceremony at the summit and the unveiling of a bronze plaque. It is the 548th site in the United States to be recognized for its exceptional natural heritage. Among the speakers and guests was Egon Pedersen of Diablo, who spearheaded the drive. He is a member of the San Ramon Valley Historical Society, and in the mid-1970s began working toward state recognition for Mount Diablo, which was given April 23, 1978. Other participants were former State Senator John Nejedly of Walnut Creek, Bob Doyle, president of Save Mount Diablo, William Penn Mott, Jr. of Orinda, president of the State Park Foundation, Mary Bowerman of Lafayette, author on the mountain's flora, and Angel Kerley, formerly of Danville, who donated her almost sixteen hundred-acre ranch on the western slopes to Mount Diablo State Park in 1980.

Chapter Four

Grande Dames

PODVA HOUSE
777 SAN RAMON VALLEY BOULEVARD
DANVILLE

The two-story home known as the Podva House had an address of 777 San Ramon Valley Boulevard, Danville. It was near Sycamore Road, at the signal light, south of downtown Danville. It was probably built about 1885.

Adolphus Godfrey Podva was born in Montreal, Canada, a French Canadian. He married Mary Alma McPherson. They had three sons: Roger L., Robert Randolph and Alfred McPherson Podva. Adolphus purchased the house from a Mr. Burgess in the late 1800s. Son Roger L. Podva and his wife Ruby May (Oswill) bought it from his mother, widow of Adolphus, in 1911. Both of their sons, Adolphus La May and Roger Oswill Podva, were born there.

Roger L. Podva died February 24, 1967. His widow Ruby lived in the home for sixty-five years before her move to the Regency Apartments on Podva Lane in April 1977.

This old Victorian-type was run down, vandalized and almost stripped of its interior *, and was doomed to destruction or removal when the Danville Livery and Mercantile Shopping Center began development and decided not to incorporate it in their plans.

They sold the house for one dollar to Doug Offenhartz and his partners, Mark Stott and Pat Lenz. Following much controversy and newspaper publicity they moved the house about 200 feet south in July 1980. It now bears the new address of 809 Podva Road, Danville. They rebuilt the foundation and made other improvements, including a handsome stand of redwood

Podva House. (Photo by Averie Cohen, San Ramon Valley Herald)

trees, hoping to convert it into a medical complex.

The current owners are Daniel K. Woodson, D.D.S.* and his wife Sande*, who have made their home on La Serena Avenue, Alamo, for four years. they have also lived in Danville and San Ramon following their move from the Los Angeles area in 1973. They have an adopted daughter Jeanette Ann, born March 6, 1981, and are awaiting a second adoption due in August 1983.

The Woodsons bought the Podva House property on its half acre in April 1982. They have spent over $200,000 and one full year's time in restoration. William T. Spencer, Jr.*, a builder and designer, contributed to the restoration project. His wife Suzan did the landscaping.

The house has been renamed the Rejoice Dental Center. It is staffed with an all-Christian personnel. Open house was held Saturday, May 21, 1983, two years to the day that the planning commission approved the renovation. James Wayne*, dental management consultant, worked with Dr. Woodson on public relations. And, quoting, the doctor said, "Saving an old house is like saving a tooth; it takes a lot of care, dedication, precision and sometimes a little pain."

*Author's footnotes: Podva House interior—only a few doors were salvaged from the Podva era. The original pair of all-wood ten-foot doors is being used and the original front door is now used at the back.

Dan and Sande Woodson grew up in Glendale, Southern California. They met and started dating in high school and continued while they attended junior college together. They were married in December 1970. Sande has a B.S. degree in education and English. Dan graduated from the University of Southern California dental school in April 1973.

William T. Spencer, Jr. is the son of Bill and Mary Spencer, my longtime friends of Danville. He and his wife live in Pleasanton with their son Christian. Another offspring is on the way. In an interview he said while restoring the Victorian farmhouse, some window trims were still available. These were preserved and used for patterns to have reproductions made.

James Wayne of Walnut Creek is related to the late John C. Wayne of Alamo. He is the grandson of Fred L. Wayne, John's brother, who built homes in Petaluma in the twenties, moved to Byron and finally settled in Oakland. He died in 1966 at the age of eighty-five. He met his wife Eleanor, a Western Electric phone operator in San Francisco, the day of the 1906 earthquake. John C. Wayne was a realtor and lived in Alamo many years with his wife Veda Verona and their son Leland.

The A. J. Young house before its restoration.

A. J. YOUNG HOME
911 SAN RAMON VALLEY BOULEVARD
DANVILLE

Albert J. Young arrived in the San Ramon Valley in 1862 and married Mary Lucinda Shuey May 3, 1868. He bought land and built this two-story Victorian home about 1870. He was a pioneer teacher and taught at San Ramon School from 1864 to 1868, Sycamore Valley School 1868 to 1879, Tassajara School 1879 to 1883 and Danville School 1883 to 1900. He was president of the Contra Costa County Board of Education from 1800 to 1902. He was also active in the Presbyterian Church as an elder, ordained May 14, 1871. He served fifty years as clerk of the session and was superintendent of the Sunday School from 1863 to 1929. The Youngs' children were Alice, Robert and Sarah H., who remained unmarried and was a teacher in Oakland and organist of the church for over forty years. Mr. and Mrs. A. J. Young died a few days after their sixty-fifth anniversary.

At one time there was a stand out front of the house from which chickens and fresh eggs were sold. After World War II a Mrs. Head from Alameda ran a residential care home there. At another time a doctor purchased it and remodelled the kitchen and redecorated.

Over the years a series of renters, good and bad, have taken over residence in the old house. It was in rundown condition when, under the guidance of Dewey D. Hinds, the commercial/industrial/land division of Geldermann Realtors, Danville, presented its plan for the Danville Medical Complex in 1980. The architect was G. Michael Golds-

10

worthy of Pleasanton. Controversy appeared, as the Contra Costa County planning staff recommended apartments or condominiums at the site. The San Ramon Valley Historical Society went on record as approving the proposed complex in a letter to the San Ramon Valley Planning Commission, dated January 16, 1980. The late Alfred B. Jones of Alamo, as its president, and his wife Virgie V. Jones, secretary of the local society, both spoke before the San Ramon Valley Planning Commission at the January 23, 1980 meeting in favor of preserving and restoring this historical building.

A cartel of Dewey D. Hinds, Tom Jackson, Ned Hoskins and Ron Johnson sold the property to Thomas F. Murphy of Alamo, in partnership with doctors who will practice at the Danville-San Ramon Medical Center at 911 San Ramon Valley Boulevard. It opened for business in June 1983.

Danville-San Ramon Medical Center general partners are Thomas F. Murphy, John K. Wilhelmy, M.D., Lynn F. Shafer, M.D., Jerome H. Davis, M.D., and Roger A. Greenwald, M.D. Limited partners are: Ryan Anderson, M.D., Davis, Shafer, Wilhelmy, M.D.s, Lee Brett Eisan, M.D., Robert Frantz, D.D.S., Roger A. Greenwald, M.D., Milton O. Kling, M.D., Edward W. Knowlton, M.D., Kim Langley, M.D., David H. Y. Lin, M.D., John J. H. Morrow, D.D.S., Alfred A. Nickel, D.D.S., Charles Glover, M.D., David Tenenberg, M.D., James Branscom, M.D., Stephen A. Reid, D.D.S., Edmund A. Schroff, M.D., Stephen and Carol Snow, D.D.S., Larry L. Stewart, M.D., Howard P. Taekman, M.D., Gary Zingg, M.D., and M.D. Properties. Fred Schrader is property manager.

Author's footnote: Mary Lucinda (Shuey) Young, born 1850, was the daughter of John and Lucinda Shuey, who in 1856 settled in Moraga. In 1858 they bought land in the Bay Area, planted fruit trees and called it "Fruitvale."

SPILKER HOUSE
1085 SAN RAMON VALLEY BOULEVARD
DANVILLE

This home, known as the Spilker house, at 1085* San Ramon Valley Boulevard, Danville, near Midland Way, surrounded by Danville Green condominiums, still remains in good repair and is still owned and occupied by members of the Spilker family. Some member of the Spilker family has

lived there since 1920. It is now on a one-acre site, part of the old ranch.

This two-story Victorian-type house was built for William Z. "Willie" Stone, son of Alamo's pioneer Silas and Susanna (Ward) Stone, and the younger brother of Albert Ward Stone. He was born March 4, 1829 at Fairview, Erie County, Pennsylvania. He married Esther Almire Stone, daughter of John Stone, January 11, 1853. They crossed the plains in 1853, the year they arrived in Green Valley, Danville. They sold the property in 1884 and bought 229 acres on the west side of Danville, and in 1885 built the house where they lived until 1903.

It later became the home of Sam and Myra Prather, who came to Danville from Oakland. Sam Prather built the Yosemite Railroad, and they were active in Danville activities.

Adolph Gustav Spilker and his wife Henrietta "Nettie" (Geiger) bought the house and farm of sixty acres in 1920 and had it remodelled for their family. They enclosed the porch and removed some partitions of the small parlor rooms. Mr. Spilker planted the walnut orchard in 1922. Their

The Spilker house, circa 1922. Five-year-old Carl is standing in front. The sign is the Diamond Grade A for walnut farmers.

11

The Spilker house being painted.

two sons were Gustav Adolph and Carl. Walter Smith was caretaker for many years. Mr. Spilker passed away in 1950 and his wife in 1952. She was president of the Danville Women's Club in 1924-25. The property was divided between the two sons. A smaller house on the property was burned.

The elder son, known as Gus, married Mary Brittan of Palo Alto, and they have two sons, Jeffrey and Jon. They were residents of this home at two different periods, first from 1950 to 1952, and again from 1956 to 1977. A swimming pool had been added about 1952, installed by Gus, who was then in the pool business. They made several remodeling additions to the home while there.

The younger son Carl is married to Jeanne Russell of New Haven, Connecticutt. They have five children: Carla, Lynnette, Russell, Mark and Keith. They lived in the house from 1952 to 1956 and again from 1977 to 1979. Their daughter Carla is married to Jamal Tayeb. They have a daughter Hanan and a son Hattan and have occupied the house since 1979. Present owners are Carl and Jeanne Spilker and their daughter and her family. They continue to restore, redecorate and upgrade this fine old home and enjoy its history.

*Author's footnotes: 1085—The author's address at 1085 Curtis Street, Albany, where I was raised and schooled for fifteen years of my life. This was my "growing up home."

Gus Spilker is a real estate broker with William F. Anderson in the Walnut Creek office, where my late husband also had his real estate start in May 1958.

Carl Spilker has operated Spilker Tree Service, Inc. since 1944, with offices in Concord.

"EL NIDO" (THE NEST) HARLAN RANCHO
19251 SAN RAMON VALLEY BOULEVARD
SAN RAMON

This lovely two-story home, for so long known as "El Nido"—the nest—in its early days was also referred to as "Harlanton" and known as the Harlan Rancho. Joel Harlan was born September 27, 1828 in Wayne County, Indiana. His parents were George and Elizabeth (Duncan) Harlan. Joel Harlan was part of the Harlan-Young wagon train which crossed the plains in 1846, part way with the ill-fated Donner Party.

On April 2, 1849 Joel Harlan married Minerva J. Fowler of Bellevue, Illinois, daughter of William and Catherine (Speed) Fowler. Their wedding was performed by Governor Lilburn W. Boggs, at the Sonoma Mission. They arrived in the San Ramon Valley in 1852. "El Nido" was built in 1858. As late as in the early 1900s, like many homes of that period, it had two front entry doors. This accommodated large families and often was a two-family* home, when a son would return with his bride. Joel Harlan died March 28, 1875.

Elisha C. Harlan, named for his uncle, was the eldest son of the nine children. He and his mother inherited "El Nido." Elisha added more acreage and enlarged the house. He died in 1938, leaving the land and home to ▬▬▬▬▬ Carmen Minerva Stolp Geldermann, who had married Al. J. "AJ" Geldermann December 1, 1928. In 1930, the Geldermanns, with a son Harlan Stolp Geldermann, left Piedmont and moved to the Harlan Rancho in San Ramon. "AJ" continued in his real estate business, selling first from out of the home.

Harlan S. Geldermann was born in Oakland. He graduated from San Ramon Valley High School in 1941 and entered Stanford University the fall of 1941. He enlisted in the United States Navy and attended Colorado College, where he was a member of the V-12 Unit. He graduated from Midshipman School at Plattsburg, New York, in June of 1944, and the U.S. Submarine Training Base at New London, Connecticut. He served aboard the USS *Spikefish* in the Pacific waters. Upon his discharge he returned to Stanford and graduated in 1947. He then became an active partner with "AJ" Geldermann in the real estate business. Their office was on Hartz Avenue in Danville, between Acree's Grocery Store and the old telephone office. "AJ" retired from active real estate business in 1953, and Harlan took it over.

El Nido (the nest) on the Harlan Ranch, San Ramon, was built for Joel Harlan in 1858. This photo was taken about 1900.

Harlan S. Geldermann married Audrey Leslie on June 30, 1950. The ceremony was held at "El Nido," the lovely mansion of Joel Harlan. Harlan S. Geldermann met an untimely death March 26, 1979 at the age of fifty-five. His widow Audrey* remains on the Geldermann property. The sons James and Joel were left the "El Nido" home with its 357 surrounding acres and out buildings. James was married to Judi Bennett on October 22, 1982, and they make their home in Blackhawk, Danville. He is with the Geldermann real estate office on San Ramon Valley Boulevard, Danville, the oldest real estate company in the San Ramon Valley. Joel Geldermann is the current resident of historic El Nido. It has been well-kept, restored, preserved and redecorated over the years.

*Author's footnotes: Two-family home—as the extended family we know again in 1983.

Taken from the words of Carmen Stolp Geldermann, in a writing of May 1, 1939: Her grandmother Minerva J. Harlan's gardens were kept in a most neat and tasteful manner. Interesting to note that it was planned and cared for by no less a personage than the ex-royal physician to the king of Sweden, familiarly known as "Old Charlie." His passion was gardening, his besetting sin "sprees" and his status a remittance man. Much service and maintenance was done by faithful "China Boys"—the Ochs and Fus and Hoys, who lived and died in loyal service of their chosen white families.

Audrey Geldermann—Moved to Round Hill in Alamo, mid-1983.

The home was part of a house tour in 1971, sponsored by the Amador-Livermore Historical Society. Its grounds have been used, over the years, for several other worthwhile benefits such as the second annual Western Night sponsored by Lafayette-Danville Cancer League, which netted $5,000 for Contra Costa Unit of the American Cancer Society, held in July 1983.

DAVID GLASS HOME
19799 SAN RAMON VALLEY BOULEVARD
SAN RAMON

David Glass was born March 4, 1818 near Hickory, Washington County, Pennsylvania to William and Priscilla (Wiley) Glass. He was married June 19, 1844 at Ottumwa, Wapello County, Iowa, to Eliza Jane Hall. She was born January 16, 1827 in Ohio, to David and Rebecca (Walker) Hall. April 1, 1850, with three wagons, five horses, three yoke of oxen and two cows, they ventured out to the Land of Promise, via the Overland Trail, arriving in Hangtown (Placerville) August 5, 1850.

David was affected with dyspepsia and other digestive troubles and was unable to work steadily in the mines. They moved on and reached Martinez on their way to Sonoma, having come through the Livermore pass by way of Altamont. There they heard of land near Walnut Creek, and made claim to 160 acres. This was the old place near

13

Alamo remembered for its excellent apples. They built a small house sixteen feet by sixteen feet in the hill between two trees, and across the road planted the first fruit orchard in the San Ramon Valley. In the fall of 1858 they sold to Austin Hammet. David Glass had the first trading post store in Alamo, in 1852.

On April 5, 1859, he purchased 740 acres of the Jose Maria Amador Land Grant from James W. Dougherty and wife, for the sum of $5,920 (although the patent from the United States Land Commission on Spanish Land Grants wasn't approved until March 7, 1862, by President Lincoln). The fall of 1858, deed dated April 5, 1859, he built the two-story Victorian with Italianate styling for $2,700 in San Ramon.*

David Glass was responsible for starting a school in the San Ramon area with his neighbor Joel Harlan. He was one of the founders of the Methodist Church in San Ramon. The Glasses raised seven children on the Glass Ranch. It was known as "Lora-Nita" Ranch, named for the two sisters, Loretta Irene and Anita Idel (Nettie). They never married and managed the ranch all their lives. Anita was killed April 17, 1922 while working on the ranch, and Loretta died in 1931. After seventy-two years, the ranch passed into other hands.

In 1932 the home was sold at auction, and with 100 acres and a frontage of 650 feet, was purchased that year by Pierre Elissondo and his wife Gracieuse. They had come from France with their son Clement* in 1922. They later purchased an additional 160 acres. Pierre, a winery foreman, planted seven acres in vineyards. They opened a restaurant in the old Victorian home, with Gracieuse serving Basque foods. A daughter Elaine* was born in the home. The Elissondos took in several foster children and raised them with their own on the ranch. When the restaurant became too much work and the house was too big for their own use, they built a smaller house close by, in 1950.

For years the old home was leased by the Sunny Hills Rest Home, and others including the Montessori School and its administrative offices. Most recently it was the New England West Antique collective, antique dealers Jack Anderson and Brad Bullard, who moved out in May 1983. Since then the San Ramon City Council has been contemplating refurbishing the old Victorian for their new San Ramon City Hall, leasing for about $2,000 per month. Much newspaper publicity has been generated.

*Author's footnotes: Pioneer David Glass died September 9, 1897 at San Ramon. He is buried in the Glass plot in the Dublin cemetery.

Two-story Victorian had several out buildings: three barns, a men's house, a granary, three hen houses, a windmill and tank house. There were hedges, ornamental trees, an orchard and vineyard.

Clement Elissondo still lives on part of the ranch.

Elaine (Elissondo) Ove lives in Walnut Creek with

This photo of the David Glass home was taken in 1983 by Jim Stevens of the San Ramon Valley Herald.

The Boone home on "Forest Home Farms" was built in 1900. (Photo by Jim Stevens, San Ramon Valley Herald)

her family, very close to her paternal uncle John P. Elissondo, whom I visited and interviewed in May 1983.

My thanks for some of this information researched May 1980 by Guerdon L. Churchill, Jr., great-great grandson of David Glass, of Valley Springs, California. And from an original family tree by pioneer Clement Rolla Glass, Los Angeles, May 30, 1897, with a note found in the preface: "It was first compiled and written partly in ink, partly in pencil by me in 1889 while at the old home place at San Ramon where I had the invaluable aid of my mother's good memory." The manuscript bears the date January 6, 1889 and is eleven typed, single-spaced pages now.

Excerpted from a letter written by Clara Isadora (Glass) Ivory to her brother Clement Rolla Glass, dated at Martinez, May 8, 1908. She speaks of having the Glass house papered and picture mouldings in every room and the halls for a cost of $100. She also put in her own cook stove, a porcelain bath and new water boiler—plumbing and all, cost her nearly sixty dollars. She also replaced the old windmill with a new Sampson Mill, new braces, platform, lace curtains, portiers, extension curtain rods and poles. She also gave her mare for which she had been offered $125 and two colts, a yearling and one two months old, to be broken —three years each was specified. She paid seventy-two dollars in advance. They charged one dollar for outside pasture.

THE BOONE HOME
"FOREST HOME FARMS"
19953 SAN RAMON VALLEY BOULEVARD
SAN RAMON

The Boone Home, known as "Forest Home Farms," was built in 1900 by Numa Sims Boone, a great-great grandson of Daniel Boone. This two-story Victorian-type home had twenty-two rooms. The handsome garden areas are lovely with cam-

ellias, azaleas, roses and huge, old trees. Two rose bushes have quite a history. They are at their fifth location in over one hundred years of life! Leland Stanford brought the roses from New York. They came around the Horn by ship, captained by Mrs. Numa Boone's grandfather, Captain Thorn. They have been planted in Santa Clara County, San Francisco and Alameda. Four large Mission fig trees and an olive were planted by the Indians. Three of these trees still remain, the olive and two large figs.

Travis Moore "Bud" Boone and his wife Ruth moved to the ranch in 1931. They lived in part of this lovely home which they remodelled over twenty-five years ago, making it into five apartments. Travis was the son of Numa Sims and Minnie (Thorn) Boone. He passed away December 3, 1981 at age eighty at the Hacienda Rest Home in Livermore, California. His widow Ruth Berry (Quayle) Boone continues to reside at Forest Home Farms. They had no children.

There are now sixteen acres remaining, with several out buildings including the old barn constructed with wooden pegs long before the home was built, and another barn, a warehouse and walnut dehydrator plant.

This ends the westside tour. I direct you back to "downtown" Danville.

MAROON (the color)

Maroon is wine
pouring into a waiting glass,
    Maroon is blood—squirting
from a wound with a splash,
    Maroon is a strawberry
that is too ripe.
    Maroon is a rose,
standing alone on a dark, summer night.

By Jennifer Nicole Jones, age 11½, 1983

THE LOON (the bird)

Swimming alone on golden pond,
I see the sudden break of dawn;
It reflects upon the dark, ring around my neck,
I flutter away in discontent.

By Jennifer Nicole Jones, age 11½, 1983

EMOTION

Emotion, my dictionary says
    is—an agitation
    strong feeling
    any disturbance
        fear, anger, disgust,
        grief, joy, surprise, yearning
How sad, also a feeling, that we
        find only three on the pleasurable side
We have joy, surprise and yearning there
To accept with heartfelt—emotion.

BUTTERFLIES

Butterflies, are like winged flowers
        most colorful of all insects
Butterflies, are good fliers
        flapping their wings and soaring
Butterflies, are kind and good and do no harm
        and aid in pollinating
Butterflies, are daytime, sunshine lovers
        while moths venture in darkness of night!
For shame the butterflies' metamorphosis
        begins with the destructive caterpillar
But how fortunate the life span of the lovely
    butterfly
        is much more lasting for our eye!
Butterflies, are free—for nature,
        Mankind and you and me.

September 1983

BIRTHDAYS—WHO NEEDS THEM?

Birthdays—Who needs them?
The one year old—marks a plateau
    his first of more to come
The five year old—ventures on
    as soon—school will begin
The thirteen year old—enters into
    the challenging age of the teens
The twenty year old—drops a tear
    when leaving the twenties
The thirty year old—winces
    at the thought of a wrinkle
The forty year old—is told
    life is just beginning
The fifty year old—is midway to a century
    but beyond, for middle age
The sixty year old—is into senior citizenry
    and maybe looking toward retirement
The seventy year old—if in good health
    is enjoying many leisurely things
The eighty year old—used to be on borrowed time
    but now may be holding his own and enjoying it
And—on and on they go
    with each year after year
    grouping into those ten years
    and each decade continues for a lifetime
With the cakes—and all the candles
    and the hope of enough strength
    to blow them out!
Who needs birthdays?—We all do!
    Think of the alternative

CALIFORNIA'S REDWOODS

California's Redwoods—
So tall and stately—
Rising up into the skies
Shading all below
How old are you?

A BROOK

What's a brook?
    Winding
        bubbling
            clear cool
                fresh sterile pure
                    pristine clean and tasty!

16

Chapter Five

Danville

DANVILLE HOTEL

The Danville Hotel was built in 1891 when the Southern Pacific Railroad came to Danville to take out the grain being grown and sent to the European markets via Port Costa. The hotel was on the corner of Short and Railroad streets and faced the railroad tracks and then, appropriately, was named the Railroad Hotel. In about 1927, when Hartz Avenue became the main street of Danville, the old Railroad Hotel was turned around to face Hartz Avenue and renamed Danville Hotel, where it has remained. For many years the old Danville Hotel was operated by Mr. and Mrs. Edward McCauley and their two daughters, Mollie and Nellie.

Later a German chef named Paul Zeibig, of San Francisco, took over the hotel and had many successes and earned national acclaim via Duncan Hines recommendation. In 1952, Russel Glenn became the owner of the then rundown Danville Hotel when it was sixty-one years old (even though newspaper articles claimed 108 years—the "stretching of time"!). Glenn redecorated the

The Danville Hotel, built in 1891 and first called the Railroad Hotel, is now part of a Danville Historic Landmark.

The Danville Hotel in 1983, now painted red. (Courtesy Walt Mitchell, Danville Hotel Historic Properties, Inc.)

building, painted it bright red with white trim and added his collection of antiques and gold rush memorabilia. He built a "Ghost Town Patio" with outdoor atmosphere reminiscent of Virginia City, Nevada. It became a popular tourist attraction. In 1959, an addition was added upstairs for Glenn's apartment and private use. Glenn sold the business in 1962, and the "new owners" removed all the outside facade additions, as they were planning to build a motel. The deal fell through and Glenn took the property back. In 1965 he added the Danville Hotel's Silver Dollar banquet room on Railroad Avenue facing the railroad tracks. (Shades of yesteryear!—Since 1976 the Danville Hotel Restaurant and Saloon.) Russel Thornton Glenn died December 16, 1982.

In mid-1976 the eighty-five-year-old Danville Hotel building and complex of other shops were purchased by Jerry E. Carter and his wife Aileen of Blackhawk and they remain current owners. The San Ramon Valley Historical Society sponsored a bronze plaque dedication on the Danville Hotel Territory, November 19, 1977.

169 FRONT STREET, DANVILLE

This two-story Victorian-type home was built by the Howard Brothers about 1866, for the Michael Cohen family, who also had a general store on the same street. Front Street was then the main street of Danville. The lumber for the house was sent around the Horn and said to be termite-free forever!

Over the years it had other owners. Among them John F. Chrisman, who sold it to Dr. Victor John Vecki and his wife Claire, who moved there in the early 1900s and remained until the late thirties, when they moved to Walnut Creek. Dr.

Vecki was Danville's first dentist, and some local residents proudly say they still have some of his fillings!

While the Veckis lived there an early movie*, "Once to Every Woman," starring Dorothy Phillips and directed by her husband Alan Holubar, was filmed at the house with the Veckis' son and daughter and other children of the neighborhood participating.

At a later date, one owner covered the board and battens with stucco and removed the ornate Victorian "gingerbread trim." When William E. and Lucile Nickerson of Alamo owned it, they leased it to a Pentecostal Church. Henry and Charlotte Neidenbach and their children lived there for a time also.

Another group had hopes of having an Art and Design Center there. Bob and Sunny Read of Fall River Mills in Shasta County purchased the property from Bill Hockins and Maureen Oestreich in

A 1980 sketch of 169 Front Street by Chris Arnott, Valley Pioneer.

169 Front Street, Danville was built in 1866. In this photo, circa 1910, are Dr. Vecki and family members.

March of 1971, and they remain the current owners. The main building has nine rooms and two bathrooms. All are used for business rentals.

*Author's footnote: The longtime rumor and "old wives tale" that Mary Pickford stayed at this home and that "Mrs. Wiggs of the Cabbage Patch" and "Rebecca of Sunnybrook Farm" were filmed there is not true. They, and several other movies, were filmed in neighboring Pleasanton. The old Whiting house and property at 627 Rose Avenue, which was owned by Sam and Lena Whiting, was the site of the motion picture, "Rebecca of Sunnybrook Farm."

ORIGINAL GRANGE HALL
233 FRONT STREET, DANVILLE

The original Grange Hall was built by Nathaniel Howard and completed November 28, 1874. It was a one-story structure facing east on Front Street, next to the schoolhouse. Its grounds along the creek were known as "Grange Park" and was not uncommon for 1,200 people to gather to attend picnics.

By 1912 the Grange needed a larger building. It formed an association with the Independent Order of Oddfellows to finance the addition. In 1912 the original one-story lodge hall was turned and lifted. The addition was built underneath, making it a two-story building, with lodge use upstairs and dining area downstairs. This building served as the social hub for the entire San Ramon Valley and surrounding area for many years. Many large gatherings and parties, including weddings and anniversary celebrations, were enjoyed there.

The building, sometimes called the Community hall, first showed movies July 21, 1923, under the direction of Will Stewart. In the 1930s the local schools used the auditorium hall for school plays, for gym use and for inter-county basketball games and dances. Former heavyweight champion boxer Max Baer of Livermore attended dances there.

Shortly after World War II, Heaton and Marge Randall* rented the first floor for a movie theater. The Oddfellow and Rebekah lodges continued to use the second floor meeting hall. The Randalls operated the Village Theater until 1968. The building and theater business were then sold to Blumenfeld Company of San Francisco. It continued as the local and only movie house in the San Ramon Valley area until October 1980. For several years the upstairs had been closed by the fire marshal as it was unsafe.

Two weeks after the last movie was shown the property was purchased by the International Church of the Foursquare Gospel, headquartered in Los Angeles. Zion Fellowship pastor is James W. Hayford, who holds three Sunday services for his over fifteen hundred members, plus counseling. Appropriately, as in its past, it is called "The Gathering Place." The building has been extensively remodelled, inside and out, and restored with many improvements.

*Author's footnote: Heaton and Marge Randall were my neighbors for several years while they ran the theatre. They lived off Camille Avenue, as I do, but across the way on Camille Court.

The Gathering Place before remodeling.

The Gathering Place in 1983, after remodeling.

FREDRICKSON HOME
172 EAST PROSPECT AVENUE, DANVILLE

The house we refer to as the Fredrickson Home, at 172 East Prospect Avenue, was once one of two quite similar homes that were at the corner of Prospect (formerly Tiger Alley) and Hartz Avenue. They were owned by a Mr. Bispo. In early

1922 when the Veteran's Hall was to be built on that corner, Bob Monroe, Danville's first barber, purchased one house and had Steve Johnson move it to the opposite corner at Front Street and East Prospect, where it has remained.

James Fredrickson (1891-1946), with his wife Annetta, called Freddie (1901-1979), and their children moved into the house in the mid-thirties. The children were: Vera (dec.), Ida, Lillis (dec.), Lois and Glen, all born in Utah, and Barbara, born in Oakland, and Roy and Clyde, who were born in Danville. The family moved to Danville from Oakland so the children could be out in the country. The family was originally from Utah and Mormons. For a time James worked for Pat Markey at the barbershop on Hartz Avenue, next to the old firehouse.* Several of the Fredricksons still reside in the San Ramon Valley and Contra Costa County.

"A Bank of America escrow paper shows this property to be at a point northside of Prospect Avenue, 300 feet from the southeast corner owned by the San Ramon Valley Bank, N. 47° 12' W. 67.12' to corner, westerly direction along property line of James Close 91.79' to point; thence So. 42° 48' E. a distance of 96.20 ft. to commencement. This being all of Lot 1 of the Maderos Addition to the Town of Danville, CCCo., State of Calif. 'Map of Maderos Addition' a subdivision property of J. C. Maderos as conveyed in a deed from J. R. Conway to J. C. Maderos, recorded in Book 361 of Deeds, page 222, originally part of the Rancho San Ramon. Map made by R. R. Arnold, Civil Engineer, June 1920. Deed dated September 7, 1934, executed by Isabel Perry and Manuel F. Perry to James Fredrickson* and his wife Annetta for the sum of $1,050. To be paid in the following manner: the sum of $15.00 or more including interest at the rate of 7%, on the 6th day of October 1934. Bank of America NT & SA charges rate of $5.00 per annum on 6th of October each year."

Ed Godoshian of Danville bought the property from Nan Rand and Jim Roos in December 1978. The old house was painted and redecorated and opened as a gift shop named Father Nature's Shed. It gained a fine reputation, stocking a full variety of coffees, teas, candies and a line of gift items. For a time the business was a partnership with Jim Soto. Later the building was leased out and the business sold to Jane Johnson of Danville, who was its manager. Jane was married and

Father Nature's Shed.

moved out of state and Ed Godoshian took the business over.

As of spring 1983 the building has gone through another renovation with removal of inside walls and partitions and opening it up to be one large room with a storage room, skylighted and very open. It now specializes in a complete gourmet line including wines and cheese. It reopened May 16, 1983.

It is a good companion to the buildings next door known as Father Nature's Gourmet Restaurant, whose main building started its life as an old goat shed taken down from the hills in Diablo. It had been used for milk storage by Basque people. That building was purchased from Robert Gould of Diablo in 1976.

Author's footnote: Building next to old firehouse used to be a bakery, now Storeroom of Gifts, 136 North Hartz, Danville.

Fredrickson—As I have said before, not all records as found in county seats are always accurate. There are often misspellings, etc. Hereto, in this deed the spelling of the Fredrickson name always carried the extra "e" and was shown as Frederickson, which is incorrect. The proper spelling was made for accuracy and clarity by the author.

ANOTHER PODVA HOUSE
100 SCHOOL STREET, DANVILLE

About 1880 the Shuey family* of Danville built the two-story provincial style house at the corner of School Street and Danville Boulevard. Subsequent dwellers were many. Among them were Roy Wells and later Mr. and Mrs. Billy Williams and their two children, who were there about 1911.

A 1980 sketch of the Podva Townhouse by Chris Arnott, Valley Pioneer.

Alfred McPherson Podva, son of Adolphus Godfrey Podva and his wife Mary Alma (McPherson), lived in the home with his wife Lilas. They had a son Alfred, Jr., who was killed in a carriage accident when he was about ten years old. After Alfred M. Podva died his widow Lilas married a William "Bill" Tarpley and they had another child. In 1923 James Close and his bride lived in the apartment. In 1928, as a young bride, Mildred Lynch (who is now Mildred Williams) and her husband, Pete Lynch, lived in the upstairs apartment while her parents, the Watsons, rented the downstairs. Soon thereafter, the Lynches purchased their own piece of Goold property.

Adolphus La May Podva, known as La May, and some call him Al, elder son of Roger La May Podva and his wife Ruby May (Oswill), with his wife Cecile (Bradley), daughter of Edward* and Hilda Bradley of Walnut Creek, purchased the home in 1938 from Mrs. Tarpley. They continued to live in Walnut Creek and rented the house out. Sometime in 1940 they moved into the old home with their daughter Marilyn and son David.

La May and Cecile Podva have remained and are still the owners and current residents.

*Author's footnotes: Shuey family—owners of a very

large dairy in Berkeley. We were their customers while we lived in Berkeley and Oakland, and Alamo for a time, when they brought home delivery out to the country in 1948.

Edward Bradley, a former mayor of Walnut Creek, was 100 years old August 1983. He now makes his home at Oak Park Rest Home in Pleasant Hill, following a stroke. He and his wife (dec.) resided in Walnut Creek since 1913.

JAMES ROOT, SR. HOUSE
310 LINDA LANE, DANVILLE

This lovely two-story older home was built by Joel Haden Boone, direct descendant of Daniel Boone, in the late 1800s. His wife was Sophie Love, daughter of Robert Beatty Love. The house was originally located on North Hartz Avenue, where the Shell station has been since 1950.

In 1910 Joel Boone's daughter, Ina Root, and her husband (June) James Root moved into the house. James Root was born December 25, 1867 and died January 28, 1948. Ina was born October 3, 1873 and died October 24, 1963. They traveled to Martinez to obtain their marriage license on the first Southern Pacific train out of Danville early in November of 1891. They were married in Danville November 5, 1891.

Their children were: James Pearley, Elmer Austin, Cora Amelia, Sara Adeline and Harold Boone Root. James, Sr. was a farmer and raised bees on the Love Ranch. He and his son Austin started the Mount Diablo Dairy in 1931, processing the milk in a building on Linda Mesa Avenue. They made home deliveries until 1945.

The Charles Ignatius Hardiman family lived in the house about 1948 while it was on North Hartz

A 1982 sketch of the Root house by Chris Arnott, Valley Pioneer.

Avenue. Shortly after it was moved daughter Eileen (Root) and her husband Robert "Mac" McCauley lived there.

Then followed a gift shop called the Treasure House, owned by a pilot who traveled and bought items that his wife could sell in the store. Later there was a music store from whose owners Leroy H. and Anne Hough of Diablo bought the building and property in the early 1960s.

On December 27, 1977 it was purchased from the Houghs by Peter Paige and his wife Judy of Alamo. Leasees were the Tree House, with children's clothing, and the Sample Cell, women's sample clothing. The main house is presently leased to the Cornucopia, owned by Barbara Price, who moved in November 1, 1982. It had been next door for seven years as an antique and dried materials store. The five rooms are now filled with dried and silk arrangements and all the materials to make them. Classes in this flower technique are also offered.

The adjoining former garage to the house has been leased to Katherine "Tanner" Sherk, as Jack's Place, picture framing.

AUSTIN ROOT HOUSE
120 WEST LINDA MESA, DANVILLE

Austin Root built this home in 1919 for his wife Elizabeth (Hansen) Root and their daughter Eileen, at the corner of Hartz and Linda Mesa, with pear orchard around it. This is the northwest corner where the Shell station is now. Their second daughter, Jean, and a son, Elmer Austin "Bud" Root, Jr., were born in the house.

In 1950, when Shell Company bought the property, the two Root houses were moved behind the station, on Linda Mesa and Linda Lane. The Austin Roots continued to live there until May 1952, when they moved into their new home on Diablo Road. Their daughter Jean and her husband Ken Witte and family lived there until about 1955.

The house was sold to Dr. Ezra Clark, the local pediatrician, and his wife Barbara in June 1959. Dr. Clark opened his medical offices in the house. On May 26, 1969, by trustees deed Barbara Clark Babb took possession of the property. She rented it for a short time to the Discovery Center. And, while it was for sale, the building was rented to others as a residence.

On October 23, 1973, Barbara Babb sold the

The Austin Root house at 120 West Linda Mesa in Danville was built in 1919. It is now Antique House.

property to Leroy H. and Anne Hough of Diablo. They leased to a series of antique shops including Primitive Junction Antiques. Barbara Price, owner of the Cornucopia, leased there for seven years until November 1, 1982, when she moved her shop next door where it is currently.

The house is now the Antique House, and the owners Leroy H. and Anne Hough operate their doll shop there. There are six rooms of dolls and everything relating to dolls and varied kinds and sizes of teddy bears.

The adjoining former garage to the house is now the Bull Pen, where years ago Jack Sherk started Jack's Place. The Bull Pen is a sports hobby shop which stocks T-shirts, pennants, caps and sports cards. Owner is Mark Kirkman of Danville, who grew up right across the street from his business. His uncle is Duane Elliott, retired fire chief.

PAT MARKEY HOUSE (MACOMBER)
217 WEST LINDA MESA AVENUE, DANVILLE

The house we now refer to as the Pat Markey house, 217 West Linda Mesa Avenue, was probably built in 1860, on the side of the hill in the Las Trampas Range, now known as Montair. It was built for the Macomber* family for whom a street was named. It probably began as a caretaker's house. Several different members of the Macomber family lived on the property, off and on, over the years. The small home remained vacant for several years as well.

In 1946 realtor John C. Wayne of Alamo sold the

A 1982 sketch of the Markey (Macomber) house by Chris Arnott, Valley Pioneer.

property to Claude Andreasen, including the small farmhouse and a barn. He had John Graham remodel it so the family could move in by 1947, where they lived with their two daughters Joan and Claudia, for four years. When Mr. Andreason decided to build a larger home he wanted the smaller one moved. Knowing that Pat Markey had some nice open, flat land below, he contacted him.

Pat and Ruth Markey bought the house in 1951 and had it moved over the hillside to settle it at 217 West Linda Mesa Avenue. It was a very hazardous trip, as there were no roads to speak of and the grade was steep. It took three tractors to get it moved—two to hold it back and one in front to lead the way down and over the hillside. When the Markeys redid some interior rooms they found some old walls were papered with an old German newspaper, including an advertisement for sarsaparilla! Pat Markey died in August 1983 at the age of eighty-two. His widow still owns the home.

*Author's footnote: Macomber family—how many remember the tall pair of metal gates set in brick that Mr. Macomber installed at the entry of Linda Mesa Avenue? They were supposed to be for privacy.

ELWORTHY HOUSE
1435 SAN RAMON VALLEY BOULEVARD
DANVILLE

Elmer Baldwin, uncle to the late Congressman John F. Baldwin* of Danville, had the two-story house at 1435 San Ramon Valley Boulevard, built in 1910. He was married to Zoe (Kemp), niece of the Reverend Symington of the Presbyterian Church of Danville. The house was designed and built by Thorup and Asmussen of Hayward (known as Haywards in those days). It was on the

site of former Laberee property where another house had been. For several years it had a San Ramon address.

In the practice of extended families, as has been returned to today, their daughter Winona (Baldwin) and her husband Herbert J. Elworthy came to live with her parents when they needed help. They had two sons while in the home, Herbert J., Jr. and Robert. They lived there until 1952 when they moved to their new home a distance away. Son Herbert J., Jr. is married to Jean Roy and they have four children and live in the Crow Canyon area. Son Robert and his wife Eunice make their home in Danville. Both sons continue to run cattle wherever green belt areas are available, i.e. Tassajara, Altamont, Pittsburg.

In 1952 Harold and Vi Frazer purchased the home from the Elworthys. Mr. Elworthy passed away in 1974. Robert L. Livermore and his wife Jean (Everett) moved into the house in 1970 from San Ramon. Their twins, Sara* and Robert, Jr., celebrated their eighth birthday there. Their two older children are Caroline and Lauren. All chil-

A 1981 sketch of the Elworthy House by Chris Arnott, Valley Pioneer.

dren attended local schools. The Livermores re-modelled the kitchen and put in a wood-burning stove. This older home is two-story with five bedrooms, two and a half baths, seven other rooms, two full basements, and a full attic with skylight. Out buildings are two sheds and a two-car garage. A new barn is planned for the future. The Livermores continue to be the current owners/residents.

*Author's footnotes: My late husband went to school with the late Congressman John F. Baldwin and his sister, Margaret (Baldwin) Wildenradt of Danville, whom I thank for some of this information. John would have been sixty-eight years old June 28, 1983, and his cousin Winona (Baldwin) Elworthy was eighty-eight years old June 29, 1983—twenty years apart.

Sara Livermore was named Miss Contra Costa 1983 at the pageant August 27, 1983. She is a twenty-one-year-old tall blonde with green eyes.

LOVE RESIDENCE
357 LOVE LANE, DANVILLE

The two-story eastern colonial home we refer to as the Love residence was built in 1860, and members of the Love family, for whom the street was named, lived there for many years. The extensive Love Ranch property surrounded the house and went up into what we now know as Montair in the Las Trampas hills.

Sam Smith, a builder, lived in the house for about one and a half years before it was sold by

Chester Love to the Woodburns of Piedmont. Ridgway Woodburn, a Bay Area contractor, and his wife Azella (Marcatos) of Piedmont, with their three children, Tom, Steve and Wendy, purchased twenty-five acres, including the old rundown house, and moved in 1950.

They discovered the old house was built on four cornerstones for its foundation. The Woodburns completely redid the home with a new foundation, rewiring and replumbing. They replaced wooden portions, took out partitions of the many small rooms and added a large room at the rear, trying to make it livable and to restore its original historic heritage. They continued to redecorate and put in a thirty- by sixty-foot swimming pool, driveways, walkways, and some Japanese garden areas. The old barn up the hill from the house, built years before the house, is said to have been used as an old dairy for many years. Several locals raised bees at the Love Ranch over the years. The Woodburns built a guest house near the old barn and sold off that portion.

The Woodburns sold off property for home-sites* to several who became their neighbors, among them Judge Richard Calhoun and his wife Darlene (Hawkinson) and their children, who built a southern colonial next door.

A movie was filmed at the Woodburn home and grounds in 1964. Mike Roberts, photographer, organized the filming and the outing. About fifty participants including children, all in full old-

The Love residence.

This 1983 photo of the Love residence with present owners Louis A. Dore and his wife Barbara standing in front was taken by Jim Stevens, San Ramon Valley Herald.

fashioned costumes, with their old classic automobiles, became "motion picture stars." Azella's beautiful antiques from indoors were also utilized. The all-day filming was climaxed with a box lunch around the pool area. Ridgway passed away in 1975. His widow married Dr. Bill Harris, a retired dentist, October 7, 1977, and they make their home in Lafayette, where I visited them the end of July 1983. They enjoy world travel along with their many other activities.

In 1965 the Woodburns sold the home to Louis A. Dore, Jr. and his wife Barbara. When the Dores were redoing an upstairs dormer attic room, making it into a studio, they found late 1850 newspapers between the walls and boards. Newspapers were often used for insulation purposes. This home has been redecorated, remodelled and restored several times, including a completely equipped poolhouse with two baths, built by the Dores.

After living in this lovely old home on its 1.69 acres for eighteen years, the Dores have it for sale listed at $625,000. The house now has 4,000 square feet in living area of three bedrooms and studio and bath upstairs, living room, dining room, master bedroom, bathrooms and kitchen downstairs, and other functional areas. Peaceful garden areas surround this home.

In October 1981, during a winter storm with seventy-mile-an-hour gales, the over-300-year-old oak tree in the side garden was hit by the strong winds. All major limbs were broken. The old tree

was six feet ten inches at its base and 120 feet tall with a spread of 120 feet. It surely is missed. The Dores purchased a one-third acre lot in Bryan Ranch and will be moving to Emmons Canyon Lane, Danville, when this house is sold.

*Author's footnote: Homesites—my late husband Alfred B. Jones, a partner of Jones-MacDonald Realtors of Danville, purchased some lots and built speculative homes in the 1960s.

At one fun function for charity at the Woodburn home how well I remember the pleasant holiday time aroma wafting throughout the house from the kitchen where cider, cloves and cinnamon simmered on the range.

SMITH RANCH
199 OAK ROAD, DANVILLE

The Smith Ranch was well established in Alamo Oaks long before this early subdivision was developed by Byington and Fagan Realtors of Alamo, in 1934. It is located at 199 Oak Road. Legal county records tell us the progression of ownerships are as follows:

1. On June 10, 1871, Peter and Anne Macauley homesteaded 160 acres (quarter section). (Book # 1 of Patents, page 275, recorded July 17, 1871.)

2. Sold by Macauley July 17, 1871 to Lawrence Smith, for whom a street was named.

3. Deeded by Lawrence to Hannah Smith, 1906.

4. Probated July 24, 1913 to five Smiths: John, Edward, Emily, William H., and Mary Kay.

5. John Smith deeded to Helena E. Smith on November 14, 1925, recorded December 3, 1925.

6. William Smith to Edward Smith, July 23, 1928.

A 1980 sketch of the Smith Ranch by Chris Arnott, Valley Pioneer.

The Smith Ranch.

7. June 14, 1934, Frank J. Byington and Edward G. Fagan bought at probate sale from Edward, Helena, Mary K., Emily Smith.

8. Edward G. Fagan conveyed his interest to Frank J. Byington, 1936.

9. Frank J. Byington sold to Delahaye, 1938.

10. Delahaye sold to J. Walter and Thelma Wellman, June 1943—3½ acres.

11. J. Walter and Thelma Wellman sold to Howard and Jean Foulds, end of 1947, and moved out January 2, 1948.

12. Howard and Jean Foulds sold to Phillis, 1948.

13. Phillis sold to Hugh and Mimi Gordon.

14. Hugh Gordon sold to Wesley and Lois Sizoo, September 1958, two acres. Sizoos renovated, made additions and improved the property.

15. Wesley and Lois Sizoo sold to Mike and Chris Roach of Diablo in 1979 and moved to Rossmoor, September 18, 1979. Current owners are Mike and Chris Roach, their daughter Kerry and son Preston Joseph, known as "PJ." The Roaches have continued to make improvements and preservation including an enlarged deck off the dining room. They have built an old-fashioned gazebo and a children's playhouse, and added an attractive picket fence. A family wedding took place in the gardens in the summer of 1983.

OSBORN HOME
928 DIABLO ROAD, DANVILLE

The 127-year-old two-story New England style home known as the Osborn Home was built by the Howard Brothers in 1856 for Joel and James Boone, descendants of the Daniel Boone family. They lived there prior to 1861. The chain of ownerships* from then to 1926 has not been determined.

In 1926 the property was purchased by I. Melvin Osborn (1880-1966). His wife Myrtle would not move out to the "wild, bleak countryside" if he did not add inside plumbing. He did, and the family arrived in April 1926. On the forty-seven acres they raised livestock—horses, cows, hogs, chickens, rabbits—and bred fine horses and participated in rodeos.

They had six children. All attended local schools and several still live in the Danville area, some on the same original property. Mr. Osborn was supervisor of roads for Contra Costa County for ten years, in the San Ramon Valley area before his retirement. He later was in the insurance business, and for a time, so was his wife. He passed away in June 1966.

Myrtle Osborn was the Danville librarian for twenty-eight years, from 1945 to 1973, when she retired. The library was one room of the Veteran's

A 1980 sketch of the Osborn house (Joel Boone house) by Chris Arnott, Valley Pioneer.

Hall when she began. Two sons, Mac D. and James Osborn, have operated Osborn Spraying Service since 1938.

Myrtle Osborn continues to reside in the home. An apartment above is rented out.

Research tells us the actual front of the house faces the creek away from Diablo Road, where the original road used to be.

*Author's footnote: Chain of ownerships—it has been said that in 1913 the house belonged to the Cooks of Diablo and a Chinese laundry was established and serviced the Diablo Country Club.

WHITE GATE FARM
40 SHANDELIN COURT, DANVILLE

This home was built in 1856 by Nathaniel and Charles Howard, popular builders of the day. It was a duplex of colonial New England design, built of logs from Redwood Canyon which were taken around the Horn to Maine, milled into lumber and returned by ship. The house included redwood mud sills, hand-cut and hand-finished doors and double hung windows and Georgia pine cupboards.

White Gate Farm was on the road from Alamo's Henry Hotel to the coal mine areas at Nortonville and Somerville. Stables and bunkhouses provided a stopover for drivers and animals. Some of the upstairs rooms of the old home were used as a school until 1865, when the first Green Valley schoolhouse was built.

In 1886-87 the property came into the possession of Judge Warren Olney. In 1898 Judge William H. Donahue and his wife Annie bought the property but continued to live in Oakland by Lake Merritt. He died in 1949. During a four-year period different people and caretakers lived at White Gate Farm. The original "Man O'War," predecessor of the racing champion, was foaled at White Gate Farm.

In 1902 John Joseph Donahue and his wife Ellen Collier (Collier Canyon, Livermore, was named for her family) lived at White Gate Farm. One of their sons, Frederick L. Donahue, and his wife Ruth Marie (Mortensen) continued to live at White Gate Farm with their two sons, Raymond Louis and Edwin P. Donahue, who were born at the home.

Raymond restored and remodeled the house for thirty years. An addition designed by his mother was added in 1970. She died September 1973 and the father in January of 1974. Raymond made

White Gate Farm was built in 1856 at Stone Valley and Green Valley roads, now in Danville.

White Gate as photographed by Jim Stevens, San Ramon Valley Herald, *in 1983.*

more additions until the house had six bedrooms with five bathrooms, large family room and laundry, plus all the other rooms to make it a large two-story home surrounded by three acres, plus swimming pool.

Raymond the son passed away October 6, 1980 at the age of sixty-one years. Named as his heirs December 1981 were Max L. Hale and his wife Janet. They remain the current owners, though the house and grounds are for sale for $535,000.

Author's footnote: John Joseph Donahue always referred to the home as "Shandelin Hall."

On September 20, 1975, the San Ramon Valley Historical Society sponsored a bronze plaque dedication honoring the builders, Nathaniel and Charles Howard, the well-known Howard Brothers.

BLACKHAWK RANCH
PEPPERWOOD LANE, DANVILLE

In 1913, Blackhawk Ranch was a portion of the 6,000 acres purchased for $150,000 by Robert N. Burgess, Sr. from Mrs. Louise Boyd, who inherited the property from her uncles Seth and Dan Cook. It was then called Oakwood Park Stock Farm of Diablo. When the Cook family owned it, it was known as the Cook or Railroad Ranch. One small part, about 1,200 acres, was sold to Ansel Easton of Hillsboro and became Blackhawk Ranch. The Blackhawk name came from his place in Hillsboro, where he raised blue-blooded stock.

This portion of the ranch was located on the southern slopes of Mount Diablo. Ansel M. Easton had the fifteen-room house built in 1916 for $50,000. The architect was Louis Muffgardt, associated with Bernard Maybeck. It was stucco of Spanish design, U-shaped, with a tower room over one entry. It had many fireplaces and eight bathrooms. Midway in its construction, it burned down, but was immediately rebuilt and completed by 1918. Ansel M. Easton and his son-in-law, William A. Ward, and their wives, both named Louise, moved into the lovely home.

In 1934 Easton sold the Blackhawk holdings to Raymond C. Force, retired president of Caterpillar Tractor Company of San Leandro. The Force family continued to reside in Piedmont, from 1934 to 1941, using the Diablo estate (Blackhawk) as a summer house. In 1941 they moved out to Blackhawk. They remodelled the home to a French decor. Seven acres of landscaped garden surrounded the large house.

In 1951 Mr. Force passed away and his widow, Florence, in 1956 sold the property to Castle and Cooke Ltd. and Helemano Company Ltd., of Honolulu. The then 6,556-acre Blackhawk Ranch sold for $1,250,000. Mrs. Force returned to Piedmont.

In 1964 G. Howard Peterson of Peterson Tractor of San Leandro bought the ranch from Castle and Cooke. Peterson did extensive remodeling, adding overhangs and heavy shake roof, replacing and adding more windows, adding eight-foot height doors throughout, lowering some ceilings and changing the entry. He was also responsible for piping in East Bay water to supplement the available supply from natural springs. He en-

Blackhawk in 1983.
(Photo by Jim Stevens,
San Ramon Valley
Herald)

larged the master bedroom wing and improved many areas, creating a 9,000 square foot house. Peterson and his wife Marion also made extensive improvements in the huge garden areas.

In the mid-1970s Peterson sold to Blackhawk Development Company*, retaining 300 acres at Blackhawk, including the house and surrounding gardens, where they resided until 1976. In May 1977 Peterson sold the home with 300 acres to Dr. Daphne Chisholm, who did remodeling to make it into a health and beauty spa to be called Renaissance West in Danville. Its potential was never realized. The Petersons moved to Round Hill, Alamo.

*Author's footnotes: Blackhawk Development Company—July 27, 1983, Owen Schwaderer was replaced as president by Walnut Creek attorney Dan Van Voorhis. The Blackhawk development, in the Mount Diablo foothills, has a population of 1,419 residents in the 550 homes now occupied. There are an additional 120 homes in some stage of construction, with half of them sold.

LEVI A. MAXCY HOUSE
4181 CAMINO TASSAJARA, DANVILLE

The Maxcy House at 4181 Camino Tassajara, six miles east of Danville, was built in 1890 for Levi Alexander Maxcy*, when he returned to the Sycamore Valley. In 1848, he and a group of men bought a sailing vessel, *The Velasco*, and sailed around the Horn to San Francisco. He had originally crossed to the Sycamore Valley in 1852. In about 1853 he married Sarah McInturf. They had

two sons, Asher and Edward, who attended Sycamore Grammar School. Neither ever married. Levi and Sarah divorced.

On December 24, 1881, he married a widow, Mrs. Rhoda (Hyde) Williams, who had a daughter Fanny. Their ancestors had come to America just a few years after the landing of the *Mayflower* in 1620.

Maxcy planted grapes and a family fruit orchard on five or six acres. He made and sold wine. About a year before his death on May 17, 1913, the vines were removed and replaced with a walnut orchard. At one time the property was 450 acres.

Fanny married James Longstreet Coats* in 1895 in San Francisco. He was later a "revenue man"* covering five counties: San Joaquin, Tuolumne, Stanislaus, Calaveras and Contra Costa, with horse and buggy or by train. Later he worked for the California Wine Association in San Francisco until he retired in 1924. On January 9, 1901 a daughter Vivian was born in the Maxcy house in Sycamore Valley. She rode horseback the two and one-half miles to the Sycamore Grammar School, and later the six miles to San Ramon Valley Union High School in Danville. The family moved to Berkeley in 1918. She attended the University of California there, taking public health nurse courses. Vivian Coats married Charles Ninian Edmonston on November 26, 1932* in Reno, Nevada. They had one son, Charles Ninian, Jr., and a daughter, Frances Ann.

There have been few tenants in the home since 1918. It was leased for farming to Manuel Santos and later to Hans Hansen and his wife and four

The Levi Maxcy house was built in 1890.

A 1981 sketch of the Levi Maxcy house by Chris Arnott, Valley Pioneer.

Camino Tassajara was tree-lined with old locust trees.

*Author's footnotes: Levi Alexander Maxcy was of Scotch descent. The American family home is at North Attleboro, Massachusetts. Many Maxcys are in that cemetery. Levi A. Maxcy is buried in the old Alamo Cemetery in Alamo.

James L. Coats died in San Leandro on September 16, 1934 and is buried in the Dublin Cemetery.

A "revenue man," a government gauger, worked for a distillery inspecting saloons for correct liquor tax stamps and testing for adulterations.

November 26, the author's birth date.

ORIGINAL TASSAJARA SCHOOL
5900 OLD SCHOOL ROAD
TASSAJARA VALLEY, DANVILLE

Isn't it wonderful to make a discovery? All these years we've thought the original Tassajara School built in 1865 had burned down. Now through research and an interview with Edward C. Rasmussen of Camino Tassajara, it has been relocated. Many years ago a Mr. Jones, who lived in the old schoolhouse, told Mr. Rasmussen about it. When it became too small for the enrollment, it was replaced with a new schoolhouse and the old building was moved a half mile east* of its original location.

The original Tassajara School was built by Albert Galatin Wilkes on his land on the left side of the road on Finley Road, near the Albert home and the Tassajara Post Office. It was built in 1865. Pioneer teacher was Albert J. Young, from 1879 to 1883. Sabra Simpson Bright from Danville was also one of the first teachers. Some of the early students in about 1878 were: Bethel, Ella and Russell Coats; Belle, Mary, Mattie, Tillie and Wilson Finley; Edgar Harris, Caroline Joseph, Annie Martin; Effie, Emma, Ernest and Willie McPherson; Ed, Lizzie and Richard Williams.

In about 1887 students were: Manuel Antone, Phoebe Bowles; Jennie, Ella and May Coats; Frank, Mary and Rose Davina; Ella Drennan; Ella and Mamie Fergoda; Abbie, Louise, Lucy, Mary and Wilson Finley; Bertha, Charlie and Willie Hanna; Augusta and Lizzie Koch; Chester Johnston, John Kroeger, Elsie, Ernest, Clarence and Nina McPherson, John Madeiros, Tony Olivera and Edward Williams. Their teacher was Richard

sons. When Hans died the sons continued the farming. The youngest son, Regner Hansen, and his wife lived in the Maxcy home until he retired in 1981 and moved to Modesto. Richard "Rick" and Carolyn Douglas are 1983 residents.

In 1961 Vivian Edmonston gift-deeded the ranch and house to her son, Charles Ninian, Jr., and daughter, Frances Ann (Edmonston) Alcalay. It is now for sale with the stipulation that the 1890 Maxcy house be preserved.

When I visited in mid-June 1983, I noted two old barns still standing and a shed formerly used for the walnut harvest. The drive to the house off

Original Tassajara School, built in 1865. The photo was taken in June 1983.

Williams, who nine years before had been a student.

It is interesting to note that there were thirty-nine school districts in Contra Costa County in the 1800s. They were divided by townships which also saw boundary changes when certain areas were too large a territory (just as it is done today). Names of those school districts were:

Alamo, Alhambra, Antioch, Bay Point, Brentwood, Briones, Carbondale, Central, Concord, Danville, Deer Valley, Eden Plain, Excelsior, Green Valley, Hot Spring, Iron House, Lafayette, Liberty, Lime Quarry, Lone Tree, Martinez, Moraga, Morgan Territory, Mount Diablo, Mount Pleasant, New York, Oak Grove, Pacheco, Pinole, Pleasant Hill, Rodeo Valley, Sand Mound, San Pablo, San Ramon, Sheldon, Somersville, Sycamore, Tassajara, and Willow Spring.

In 1865-66 the combined enrollment of all schools in the Alamo-Danville-San Ramon area was 131 pupils!

Over the years the original Tassajara School has had several additions and many residents. It became a part of a 160 acre ranch and was called "the bunkhouse."

On February 7, 1944 the 160 acre ranch belonged to Edward C. Rasmussen, who bought it from the Azevedo family at a court sale. In 1969, Robert Pierre Raskob* and his wife Dolores bought the 160 acres from Ed Rasmussen. The property had been leased for cattle, hay and grain. The Raskobs used it for cattle running and a quarter horse ranch. They built a large house on the hill

overseeing the ranch and overlooking the entire valley. Mr. Raskob passed away in 1974 and his widow did a mini-subdivision and in 1978 sold to Mike Steele and Bill McLaughlin.* Mr. Steele is in the insurance business with offices in San Francisco. They have refurbished the entire ranch and named it Avondale Farms, Inc. for thoroughbred breeding, training and racing. There is a five-eighths mile training track with swimming pool for the horses. The grand opening celebration was Monday, July 4, 1983, with a reception at 6:00 P.M. and dinner at 7:30, followed by 8:30 entertainment and dancing until 11:00 P.M. All proceeds went to support the Equine Benefit, women's auxiliary of the Horsemen's Benevolent Protective Association, a non-profit national organization.

The old schoolhouse is having a facelift and will be used as a clubhouse for owners and trainers. It is near a large stand of old eucalyptus and a row of oaks.

*Author's footnotes: Half-mile—When I visited the ranch June 21, 1983, I noted that was a pretty long half mile and decided it was "as the crow flies!" Mr. Rasmussen, my guide, said it was fence-to-fence property measurement.

Robert Pierre Raskob was one of thirteen children (nine girls and four boys). He was raised in Delaware and Pennsylvania. He was named for Pierre Samuel du Pont, who had no children and was happy to share. Dolores Raskob spends much time visiting the Raskob families and their children each year.

Mr. Rasmussen and his son Gordon had reroofed the original Tassajara school years ago and mentioned that the upper section of the building had old newspapers on the walls for insulation. Bill McLaughlin had a hired hand climb a ladder to see what was there and he found a newspaper with the dateline July 16, 1891. Bill McLaughlin is a history buff and comes from an El Cerrito pioneer family.

During all the years the Rasmussens owned the ranch the old schoolhouse building was always rented and occupied—for as little as ten dollars per month for a time!

TASSAJARA SCHOOL
1650 FINLEY LANE
TASSAJARA VALLEY, DANVILLE

The second Tassajara* School was built in 1888 and the one-room building, with cloakroom at the front and two anterooms with the library in the center, at the rear, is still standing. The rear steps are missing. But the two out buildings with stalls for horses or carts remain on the one-acre plot.

This photograph of Tassajara School, built in 1888, was taken in June 1983.

The perimeter is planted with large black walnut trees which were planted by the students many years ago. There is also a row of walnut trees leading to the front door on each side. Various trees were named by the students who tended them. There is a very large one still said to be Roger Podva's.

Some pioneer teachers were: Miss Emily Stetson, 1890; Ellen A. Riley, 1891; Margaret Bowles, 1892; Will McPherson, 1893; Cora Boone, 1894; Jennie Boswell, 1895; Miss Jones, 1896; Miss Maude Merritt, 1897. In 1900 there were two teachers, Maude Merritt and Minnie Harris. Miss Ellen A. Riley returned again in 1901 and taught until 1912. Miss Denyke was the teacher in 1912-13.

A teacher in 1919, Grace Sampson Corbett, on February 12, 1919, traveling by train bound for Pleasanton, was met in his model T Ford by John Rasmussen, clerk of the school board. She boarded at the Peterson home at the junction of what later became Finley Road and Camino Tassajara. When she first viewed the little school it was like a jewel in a parklike setting surrounded by huge black walnut trees which had been planted by the children years before. On February 13, 1919, she opened the school to twenty-five to thirty pupils, grades one to eight. The students arrived and departed the school in varied transportation: horseback, carts, buggies and buckboards.

Mrs. Victor Edward (Grace Sampson) Corbett, later when widowed, returned to the Tassajara Valley July 3, 1974, to live just behind the old school. Her daughter and son-in-law, Victoria and Robert T. Wright, built their new home in 1970 on acreage and named Old School Road.

In the spring of 1971, the Danville Women's Club held an historic display and picnic luncheon there. The old school bell, which had been stolen, was replaced by the last school teacher to teach there, Mrs. Arendt. The bell was from her father-in-law, who had been given the bell for selling the most war bonds. It is still there.

The Tassajara School is owned by Contra Costa County and governed by the Board of Tassajara Fire Commissioners, made up of five members. The district was formed in 1969, and Warren L. Reinstein was appointed its first fire chief. He served until his passing in February 1979. Steve Eppler of Finley Road was appointed March 7, 1979 and serves currently.

Presently fire commissioners are: Vera Reinstein, chairman, Charles Phinney, Ken Roberts, Don Carter, and Steve Morgan, who was appointed July 12, 1983. They meet the second Thursday of each month.

Recently through volunteer work and donations for materials, a new cement foundation was installed and the building shored and leveled.

Elections are held in the building as well as meetings of 4-H groups, and once a year there is a summertime barbecue on the grounds. At the end of July 1983 the outing was a fund-raiser to be used toward restoration of the old school. This school building, in its picturesque setting, has been the subject for many artists over the years.

°Author's footnotes: Tassajara (Tahs-sah-hah-rah) is from Tasajera, a place where strings of beef or venison (jerky) are hung out in the sun to dry—a word often used by the Spaniards in place-naming, with variations in the spelling.

My thanks to Mr. and Mrs. Edward C. Rassmussen of Camino Tassajara, with whom I've had interviews in June 1983 and a personally conducted tour of the area June 21, 1983.

This private residence was formerly Green Valley School.

GREEN VALLEY SCHOOL #2
1591 GREEN VALLEY ROAD, DANVILLE

The first Green Valley School was built in 1865 on a knoll opposite what later became Cameo Acres, near Green Valley Road and Blemer Court in Danville. It was surrounded by eucalyptus trees and was one of twenty-six elementary schools in Contra Costa County. The school year was July to October and again from February to June, to avoid the miserable rainy weather of winter. The enrollment was thirty-eight white children and one Indian child, ages five to fifteen. This school was valued at $575 and considered the third most valuable educational structure in the county. The teacher was Mrs. Cecelia (Henry) Gifford, who came to school in a horse and buggy from Alamo and received a salary of fifty-eight dollars per month.

Part of the school time was spent hauling water up to the schoolhouse that had been pumped by hand from a well. The "drinking fountain" was a bucket and dipper. Also wood had to be gathered and toted for heat.

The second Green Valley School and the subject of this piece was constructed, after the original one was condemned, in 1922* by builder Steve Johnson. It was an improvement over the first as it had electric lights and a large coal stove. Water

was piped into the school from a pressure pump. However, seldom was there enough water to have any pressure, and wood and coal still had to be carried up the hill to the schoolhouse—and the ashes down the hill to be dumped.

In those early days all eight grades were taught in one room. Supplies were purchased by the students until later when the school district supplied the texts. Subjects were reading, spelling, penmanship, geography, grammar and United States history.

Miss Donahue, aunt of Ray and Edwin Donahue of White Gate Farms, was a teacher. The Donahues attended Green Valley School, as did Walter Xavier and a Macedo, among others. It was said that the school closed during the depression because of less than five in daily attendance.

The building was sold for delinquent taxes in Martinez. It has been said that Curtis Haskell, town constable of Danville, purchased it for $600, with one and one-tenth acres of ground. Curtis and Gertrude Haskell lived there a few years and while there partitioned some rooms. A well was dug, but the water was unfit for drinking.

Eric E. and Lydia Turner, who had purchased the hardware store on Hartz Avenue from the Haskells in 1944, bought the former old school building from them in 1945. In 1950 Bill Diehl, Danville architect, designed the exterior remodeling and Mr. Peterson of Diablo was the contractor. The Turners lived on and enjoyed the unique knoll with its 360-degree view for thirty-one years. Everything on the grounds they planted except the eucalyptus trees and one valley oak tree. The home was sold to Ted Larson in 1976 when the Turners moved to Santa Rosa, where they remain.

*Author's footnotes: I have made an exception and used this building even though it was built after 1920, because I wanted you to realize how older buildings have been salvaged and utilized and not torn down quickly, as they seem to be in more recent years. Also, one of the former students of the first Green Valley School, Andy Andersen of Camino Tassajara, is of the belief that a portion of the original school was used in the construction of the second.

My thanks to Lydia Turner for sending me material on the Green Valley schools in the form of newspaper clippings as well as her personal notes.

Mrs. Gifford later taught at the Alamo Grammar School. I too had a teacher by that name when I attended Berkeley High School. She was Miss Gifford and she taught art.

33

PURPLE

(For Claudia Mauzy Nemir and me)

Purple—is a color
  one I hold dear
Purple—is red and blue
  and can be hues of
  lavendar, magenta, lilac,
  mauve, orchid, violet,
  grape,
And by whatever style and
  mode color
  of the spectrum
  is popular of the day
  and for the season
Purple—is for royalty
  it shows rank and station,
  authority, emperialness,
  and power!
Purple—is not just for old ladies
  with gray or white tresses
  as believed for so long.
Purple—is an important color
  in all rainbows
  and helps hold up the arch
Purples—are made of cosmic rays
  vast and grandiose!

RAINBOW

Rainbow, Nature's own
Arching across the sky
Made of moisture and sun rays
With your myriad of colors
Always, purple, blue, green,
  yellow, orange and red
Is your pot of gold treasure
The colors to the eye?

SPRINGTIME

Spring is . . .
  branches sprouting—
  buds popping—
  sun shining—
  breezes blowing—
Spring is . . .
  robin's song—
  crocus and tulips bright—
  clear, sunny days—
  warm, still nights—
  Mother Nature reborn.

HOUSEWORK . . .

Housework is a maudlin task
  Dusting, vacuuming, mopping
    and the windows to be squeegeed
Remember—when Monday was wash day
    Tuesday was ironing time
    Wednesday was for mending
    Thursday was for baking
    Friday was for cleaning
    Saturday, off to market
    Sunday, for rest and the Sabbath
And now, in more modern times
  with push buttons and power
Every day and any day
  can be for the chores
When—they fit into our busy calendars
And so much the better for us all
Housework is always there
  and more to come!

GOLDFISH

Goldfish—have some life!
  or the lack of it
Goldfish—spend their time
  going round and round a bowl
Goldfish—see you, as you see them
Goldfish—I'm afraid to say
  are poor fish!

MOUNT DIABLO

Mount Diablo, shrouded in fog—mystery
Mount Diablo, snow-capped—crisp
  and clear
  white and pristine
Mount Diablo, fluffy clouded
Mount Diablo, with its rosy glow
  or with moods of purples
Mount Diablo, we love you.

SCHOOL DAYS

School days—
  today and yesteryear
    are few and far between
No more ruler—
No more rote—
No more Palmer's penmanship
  and read the difference!

Chapter Six

San Ramon

SAN RAMON— HOW IT GOT ITS NAME

Some research says the name was first given to the creek by a "mayordomo" of Mission San Jose whose name was Ramon and who had the care of some sheep* there a long time ago.

The progession of names was:

1. Brevensville after Brevens, a first blacksmith.
2. Lynchville after William Lynch, pioneer.
3. Limerick by its Irish immigrants, not to be outdone by neighboring Dublin.
4. As it remains today, San Ramon—for its creek*, and some research shows for a Spanish saint named Ramon.

*Author's footnotes: In the memoirs of Jose Maria Amador he says the San Ramon Creek was first named El Arroyo del Injerto, injerto meaning a grafting tree. There was a huge oak tree there and from its side grew a willow tree, as if grafted there. Later it became El Arroyo de San Ramon.

In the early days, sheep from Mission San Jose grazed throughout the San Ramon Valley.

WIEDEMANN HOME
2301 NORRIS CANYON ROAD, SAN RAMON

The original Christian Wiedemann two-story Victorian farmhouse in San Ramon was built in 1865, on what had been government land. In those days some veterans were given land grants. The

The Christian Wiedemann home, built in 1865, at 2301 Norris Canyon Road, San Ramon.

This photo of the Wiedemann home and original outbuildings was taken in 1982 by Jim Stevens of the San Ramon Valley Herald.

hill land was purchased by three partners: Christian Wiedemann, Henry Schwerin and his brother. Christian Wiedemann married Catherine Dittmer. Their children were Mary, Henry, Rose and Fred. They raised hay, grain, grapes and a fruit orchard with several types of apples.

Mary and Rose Wiedemann, maiden sisters who never married, traveled the over-half-mile to Norris Canyon Road and beyond for all their needs, by horse and buggy. They raised turkeys and sold the eggs for their income. Mary died in the 1950s and Rose in 1961, never straying very far from the ranch. For a time, over the years, their niece Alberta Smoot, daughter of Henry Wiedemann, lived at the home and later visited often.

In 1963 came Bob and Pat Lenz with their two daughters, Robin and Louisa, and son Michell, who leased the property. They made many improvements, inside and outside, to preserve the old Victorian farmhouse. Added were a skylight, sliding doors, and other redecorating, and they lived in the house until 1973.

It was then that Fred Wiedemann's granddaughter Roxanne "Roxie" (Wiedemann) Lindsay and her husband Randolph "Randy" Dale Lindsay began restoration which took them over a year to complete. They moved in for Christmas in 1974 and have remained. They finished the two upstairs bedrooms after they had moved in. One is their master bedroom in which they used aged barn wood taken from a nearby old barn, and the other is for their daughter Mattie Alice, born January 29, 1977. They took out the sliding doors and replaced the pair with wooden French doors, added a bay window with window seat, remodeled the kitchen with its wood burning stove and redecorated throughout, but left the quaint

and comfy feel for the Victorian period that it was built.

Though all the trees and bushes have grown over the years, all the original out buildings are still standing. There are two granaries, a milk house, tank house, several sheds for wood, storage and chickens, and of course an "outhouse." The house has a partial basement and attic space. Presently, the house sits on five acres. Spring water from the surrounding rolling hills gives the house and grounds their water.

This home has always been in the Wiedemann family. And with Roxie's sister Sandy and her husband John La Violette, and her brother Jeff and his wife Nancy (Boggess) Wiedemann and their two sons living close by this quiet area surrounded by rolling hillside could be called "the Wiedemann Compound."* Randy and Roxie Lindsay, current owner/residents, have many more plans including new decking and extending the porch. They will continue to restore, preserve and improve on a house that has had tender love and care. They also are busy operating their business, Wallpaper on Wheels, with Randy's paper wagon of designer wall coverings.

*Author's footnotes: How well I remember the annual Round-Ups held on this section of the Wiedemann ranch. The delicious food was always served from the grounds of this old and lovely home with its special view of Mount Diablo. When I revisited in mid-June of 1983 all those memories returned.

"The Wiedemann Compound"—Their mother, Doris Wiedemann, also lives on Norris Canyon Road, but a bit removed. A paternal aunt, Ann M. (Wiedemann) Kaplan, and her husband Al live on Norris Canyon Road, and could be included.

Chapter Seven

Diablo

DIABLO

How it got its name—probably from the mountain. However, the Diablo community living did not spring up until 1914. A group headed by Robert N. Burgess, including George W. Ammens, Arthur Breed, Harlow Bancroft and E. B. Bull, changed the name to Mount Diablo Country Club in the 1914 reorganization. Reincorporation of the area in 1936 changed the name to Diablo Country Club. As late as 1939 its name was Diablo Country Club, with fifty-three homes there.

MOUNT DIABLO

How it got its name—there have been many names, with as many versions. The Costanoan Indians, the first inhabitants, called the mountain "Kah Woo Koom," which meant "laughing mountain" or "mighty mountain." In the 1840s early American explorers named it Monte del Diablo. Erroneously, they thought Monte translated to mountain (some even today believe that), when actually in Spanish it means "thicket" or "woods." Monte Diablo was used for the name of an Indian village where we now have Concord. The Spaniards called it "Sierra de los Bolbones" after the Indians. General Mariano Guadalupe Vallejo in 1850 gave the California Legislature the story of the "devilish spirits" we've all heard so many times. A San Francisco newspaperman in 1916 said he named the mountain "Koo Wah Koom" to help a real estate development in sales not to be hindered with the devilish name. To this day campers tell stories of ghostly apparitions and sounds. These can be accounted for by the sun's rays through fog banks making shadows, and when temperature, sun, air and climate are just right—or could it be wrong?

By whatever stories we apply to its name Diablo—dee-AH-bloh—has a nice tone to it and I prefer it to its Spanish translation. It is the most important landmark for all of Contra Costa County and miles beyond. When traveling, whenever I see it I know I am not far from home.

ORIGINAL DIABLO COUNTRY CLUB INN 1925 ALAMEDA DIABLO, DIABLO

Britton and Ray, San Francisco lithographers, as early as the 1850s owned the area we know as Diablo Country Club. They sold to Urial Huntington and later, about 1870, it became the property of W. W. Cameron, whose wife was Alice Marsh, daughter of pioneer John Marsh. He sold the property of about thirteen hundred acres in 1876. In 1877, Western Development Company, which was a holding company owned jointly by the Southern Pacific and the Central Pacific railroads, took it over and put John Miller, secretary of the Southern Pacific Company, in charge. He built a home there and it was known as Railroad Ranch. After the death of Miller, David C. Colton, affiliated with the Western Development Company, took over. He added many out buildings and also entertained lavishly. He was thrown from a horse and later died of blood poisoning in the fall of 1878.

In 1878 the property was inherited by Colton's daughter Carrie, the wife of Dan Cook of San Francisco. Upon her death a year later, the property became Cook's. He built a large dairy, several barns, a race track, billiard hall and reservoir. He imported prize-winning cattle and the finest race horses. He also built a new two-story home, a stately Victorian type, consisting of sitting room, dining room, office, kitchen, nine bedrooms and a dressing room. (This is the oldest building in Diablo.) His death in 1881 ended his dreams of more extensive improvements. The property was then acquired by his brother, Seth Cook, a bach-

A 1914 photo of the original Diablo Country Club Inn, built in about 1878.

elor. The acreage was 5,000 acres but was increased by buying up nearly all the small farms in Green Valley, and it became known as Cook Farm. Seth Cook died at the age of fifty-nine on February 26, 1889. His only heir was his niece, Louise A. Boyd of San Rafael. She changed the name to Oakwood Park Stock Farm, and her husband, John F. Boyd, became the manager.

Robert Noble Burgess, Sr. of San Francisco purchased the ranch of about six thousand acres for $150,000 in 1913. He started a real estate development of beautiful homesites for summer dwelling. He constructed a toll road to the top of Mount Diablo and transformed the old Cook mansion into an inn for tourists. Visitors came from all of the Bay Area cities via automobile or train. William Randolph Hearst became interested in the Diablo development in about 1914-15. Part of his contribution was in the form of national advertising in Hearst publications. These included the automobile races held from Oakland to the summit of Mount Diablo. At one time Hearst wanted to build a home on Mount Diablo similar to his mother's home in Pleasanton. The Diablo real estate development was called Mount Diablo Villa Homes and included Oakwood Park Stock Farm, then totaling about thirteen thousand acres. One small part, about twelve hundred acres, was sold to Ansel Easton from Hillsboro and became the start of Blackhawk Ranch. Following World War I sales decreased.

Burgess remodelled the inn with an "Italian villa" flavor—broad verandas, enclosed dining room, a solarium, lounge and ladies' buffet. He installed French doors and polished wooden floors to be used for dancing. In the summer of 1919, because of unfavorable post-war and other circumstances, he filed bankruptcy and moved to Walnut Creek.

Before the crash of 1929, weekends in the summer held activities at the inn. In 1931 it was in use for meals for the club members and offered some entertainment. In 1936 the depression years forced some club members to give up their memberships, and Diablo Properties, Inc. was organized. From 1938 to 1941 entertainment and dances at the inn continued. During the war years with gas rationing many problems came, and Diablo Properties, Inc. was unable to finance and continue. Their largest stockholders, Robert Hall and Herbert Hills, bought out the other stockholders.

On April 29, 1948, Laurence "Larry" Curtola bought them out and took over. The old inn was run down, so he made many improvements, remodeling and restoring it, to convert it into his private home. He and his wife Betty and their daughters lived there until 1972, when they sold it to Peter J. and Charlene Decker, current owners.

Now, in 1983, this 6,000-square-foot Victorian stately manor is for sale at $798,000. It was built with a piazza completely around three sides. It has ten- and twelve-foot ceilings, french doors, five fireplaces, some from the Cowell mansion in San Francisco; sixteen chandeliers, one imported from Venice, Italy; an eighteen by thirty-seven foot living room, dining room, four bedrooms with four and one-half baths, large family room, and kitchen with wet bar. This home has many special features, including embossed brass doorknobs with Victorian patterns. Some of its early construction has old-fashioned square nails. The house is on close to a one-acre parcel with swimming pool and barbecue areas, surrounded by stately oaks, pines, redwoods, palms and bay trees. Over the years, its owners have redecorated, remodelled and restored, to keep this one of Diablo's lovelier homes, retaining its historic prestige.

38

The original Diablo Country Club Inn in Diablo. Photo by Jim Ketsdever of the Valley Pioneer.

GARDENS

Gardens are Mother Nature's masterpieces
Gardens can be formal—or informal
Gardens can be nothing but work
    and expense—or natural
Gardens can be places with signs
    "Don't step on the Grass!"
            or
    "Do not tread here"
            or
Gardens can be
    Open—and giving and
        calm and relaxing
        places of serenity and tranquility
For you and for me—and for the weeds!

LITTLE GIRLS

Little girls—
They say, are made of
    Sugar and Spice
    Ribbons and bows
    Ruffles and lace
    Braids or curls
They are—
    Freckled or dimpled
    Cuddly or crinkled
The apple of Daddy's eye!

A MEADOW

A meadow—is an open field,
        never fenced or bordered.
A meadow—may have tall flowing grass,
        or it may not.
A meadow—with some trees,
        is a plus for shade.
A meadow—long and level,
        can be a field for kite flying.

POETRY

Poetry, my teacher always said,
Had to be in rhyme
And have meter
Nowadays,—I find
It's often words on paper.

OH THOSE GOLDEN ROOTS—
THE CARROT!

Carrots—our mothers told us
    would give us rosy cheeks,
    curly hair—even if it was already curly!
Carrots—our doctors say
    will aid our eyesight
    especially at night
Carrots—in stick form
    are for dieters
    "Chew a carrot, instead of a sweet!"
Carrots—are a lovely color
    when tossed with greens
Too many carrots will give us carrotene
    and make our skin jaundice
Carrots—are for Bugs Bunny
    and his family—not necessarily mine!

CATS

If dog is man's best friend
What's a cat?
    Shy and independent
    Patient, for hours on end
        Watching ground movement
        Fluttering of a butterfly
            Flying insect or bird
        Can relax and snuggle and snooze
            almost anywhere
                purring contentment
        And, somehow tell his needs
            and wants—when he wants
That's—a cat.
His own best friend—and yours?

ELEPHANTS

Elephants—I like elephants
    No matter if they are
        Indian or African
        whatever their ethnic background.
Elephants—I like elephants
    But mostly in statuary
        or art objects
        or curio pieces
        or even at the zoo!
Elephants—I like elephants
    Why shouldn't I?
    I'm a Republican!

Chapter Eight

Alamo

Alamo is the Spanish name for the poplar, a species of tree found in abundance in the valley and creeks that flow through it. The early Spanish settlers named the town of Alamo.

HENDRICKS HOUSE
112 EL PORTAL ROAD, ALAMO

The "Hendricks House" was built on a bit over one acre portion of Rancho San Ramon at the corner of Danville Boulevard. This property historically is a part of "Hemme Park," the original vast holding of August Hemme, and just south of his former mansion.

The German Savings and Loan Society, a corporation, took over the parcel of land in a deed dated May 22, 1914, recorded June 5, 1914, deeded to Josiah Boucher.

The two Kendall brothers, who owned a lumber business in Oakland, built a small weekend cottage on the property closest to the corner and it became 112 El Portal Road, Alamo. This small wooden structure might have been built about the time they built the two homes across El Portal, on what is now Sunset Nursery property, about 1914.

In the early 1930s came the Hendricks family from Berkeley—Lionel L. Hendricks and his wife Madaline G., with sons Bruce and Bill and daughter Barbara. Mr. Hendricks was in the real estate business with Mason McDuffie in Berkeley. They added to the structure with additions to the west side and top, making a second story. Most of the structural additions were done by them on the small original lean-to cottage. On August 30, 1941, the property was deeded to Madaline G. Hendricks following a divorce. She had a small brick house built to the east, leaving seven-tenths of an

A sketch by Chris Arnott of the Hendricks house in Alamo. (Courtesy of Michael Krajic)

41

acre on the corner. On August 6, 1946, she sold the home to George R. Handshy and his wife Helen* (Walker) and their three children, sons Arden and Tom and daughter Janie. Tom was a small baby when they lived there.

It is believed Handshys sold to the Stewart family who resided there many years. They sold to a couple who lived there about one and one-half years and who in turn sold to Paul Kintcher and his wife Joan, in 1969. Kintchers lived there ten years with their daughter Melissa and son Brad. In August 1979 they sold to Steve and Kim Arnold, who on March 4, 1982 sold to Greg and Pat Saunders, who are the current owners.

*Author's footnote: As Helen Walker from Watsonville, she was a former teacher at Alamo Grammar School.

HEMME FARMHOUSE
924 DANVILLE BOULEVARD, ALAMO

August Hemme was born in Neusadt-am-Rubenbergan, Hanover, Prussia, January 10, 1833. He was the son of William Frederick and Mary Ann (Stunkel) Hemme. William died in 1868 and his wife in 1842. August was a good scholar and when eleven years old took high honors at high school and took courses to enter the Military University at Hanover. However, letters from an older brother in the United States caused him to wonder

The Hendricks house in Alamo.

at the "New World." He set sail and landed in New York in 1846, and worked in his brother's store for three years.

When gold was discovered Hemme came west, in May 1849, mining on the Feather River with good returns. He also made money in cattle selling at the mines. He wandered to the San Ramon Valley and in 1852 purchased 2,000 acres of very fertile land on the southern end of Alamo. He later added another 1,000 acres to his property. He married Minerva Elizabeth Ish, the daughter of a neighbor farmer on January 20, 1856. The Hemme mansion was of architectural splendor, surrounded by handsome landscaping, including fruit orchards, grapevines, trees and pasture hills. It was called "Hemme Park."

A 1982 sketch of the Hemme farmhouse by Chris Arnott, Valley Pioneer.

Hemme's philanthropies were many and universal. He gave thousands toward church benefits and schools. He was classified as an early cattleman in 1860. In the spring of 1879 he was responsible for the tree planting along Danville Boulevard, and he was an active participant in bringing the railroad to the San Ramon Valley. He was an elder of the Danville Presbyterian Church starting February 7, 1886.

Heavily burdened with mortgages and the farm depresson of the 1890s, he was driven to declare bankruptcy in 1898. He left the San Ramon Valley in 1902 and moved to Berkeley, where he died in 1904. His wife passed away February 5, 1907. They are buried in the Elks Plot of Mountain View Cemetery, Piedmont Avenue, in Oakland.

The one-bedroom cedar farmhouse is said to be a part of the original Hemme estate and to have been built in the late 1800s. This farmhouse was probably used as quarters for hired help as it was close to the old mansion that burned in the early 1900s. Adjoining are buildings that were bunkhouses.* An old tankhouse was removed ten years ago.

At one time this property belonged to Emory Smith*, who was a world-wide traveler who brought trees and plants to his acreage in Alamo from all corners of the world. He carefully labeled each plant with its botanical name, species and origin, and created a miniature "Golden Gate Park" for all visitors to enjoy. It was known then as "Danala Farms," as it is known today, though the garden areas are mostly gone and homes have been built.

Robert and Fern McHale of Arcata, California purchased ten acres from Emory Smith in 1944, including the small white farmhouse. Arven R. Scott and his wife Madge (Reid) bought almost three acres from the McHale family in 1945, including the buildings which are rented out. Arven Scott is a son of Charlie Scott, who was born in the Tassajara area, and his wife Matilda (Stark), born in Alamo. The Scott family ranch was near Clipper Hill Road in Danville. Arven's twin brother Arlen lives in Honolulu, Hawaii.

Renters over the years have been many and varied. Currently, since September 1981, they are Jim and Sherry Ketsdever and their daughter Megan. Jim is photographer for the *Valley Pioneer* (newspaper) in Danville. They have screened in the front porch, partitioned and painted, and now are working on the landscaping.

*Author's footnotes: Bunkhouses—Only one remains, called a "bachelor's pad," which has been rented by Sam Kirby for about sixteen years.

Emory Smith—I knew him well and enjoyed tours of his beautiful gardens way back in the late 1930s when my mother-in-law Flora May (Stone) Jones introduced me to him because of my love of flowers and plants.

GORDON BALL ESTATE
300 CAMILLE AVENUE, ALAMO

The Gordon Ball estate was built in 1914 for the Walter Arnstein family. He was president of the Sacramento Northern Railroad. It was a large two-story mansion of its day. Originally its front entry faced west and the Las Trampas Range, where it is nestled.

The second owner was the Hutchison family, who were in the construction business. Mr. Hutchison met a tragic end transporting some dynamite near the Broadway Tunnel, as he was returning home. The Bert Raleys were the next owner/residents and they added the playhouse and the bar. The bar is part of one from the Comstock Room of the Palace Hotel in San Francisco. Mr. Raley was vice-president of Palmolive-Peet Company.

The fourth owners were Gordon H. Ball and his wife Dorothy (Griffin), who arrived July 4, 1946. Their children were G. Nathan, Dennis, Stephen and Susan. Daughter Marsha was born after they had lived in the house for a while. Gordon H. Ball Company constructed roads, airports, dams and the Oakland tunnel for Bay Area Rapid Transit (BART). In 1949 the Balls put in a swimming pool in an area which had been a fruit orchard. They also changed the original entry to face Mount Diablo to afford a gorgeous view of the mountain. Other remodeling and improvements have been made over the years to preserve this lovely home. Mr. Ball was from Porterville and raised in Berkeley. All their children attended Alamo schools and graduated from the San Ramon Valley high school. Some with their families have continued to live in the general area.

*Author's footnotes: One of the caretakers some years ago had a daughter with the melodious name of Serena Siccora.

43

Camille Avenue was named for Camille Grosjean, who owned much property on both sides of Camille Avenue. The husband of Susan E. Grosjean, he died April 30, 1906. The family resided on Las Trampas Road. One of his sons was also named Camille. His will was dated August 12, 1897.

MACFARLANE HOUSE
1206 DANVILLE BOULEVARD, ALAMO

The house we remember as the MacFarlane house was built in 1906 for the Van Gorden family. It is on one acre plus, on the east side of Danville Boulevard, near Hemme Avenue, and is included in "Judge's Row." Judge Horace Van Gorden (dec.) lived there with his mother and later his wife Charlotte and their two daughters, Betty Ann and Peggy, who attended Alamo Grammar School. The family always referred to the house as "Old Home."

The popular candy maker from the Bay Area, "Scotty" MacFarlane moved out to the country with his family, until the mid-fifties. In March 1957 Dean S. Frazier and his wife Frances purchased the house and property from Mrs. MacFarlane after her husband had died following a bad fall. The Fraziers' daughter Diane was then three years old. They moved from Gregory Gardens, Pleasant Hill, where they had lived for seven years, coming from San Leandro. Diane attended Alamo Grammar School, Rancho-Romero, Stone Valley and graduated from San Ramon Valley High School.

Over the years redecorating, upgrading and improving have been done. Dean and Frances Frazier remain as current owners and residents.

The MacFarlane house at 1206 Danville Boulevard in Alamo was built in 1906. This photo was taken in 1983.

Judge Wood's house circa 1905.

JUDGE WOOD'S HOUSE
1272 DANVILLE BOULEVARD, ALAMO

The strip along what we now know as Danville Boulevard in Alamo, which was Route 21 and the main thoroughfare north to south before the freeway, over the years has been verdant and attractive. In the early 1900s East Bay city people came out to the country for its beauty and restfulness. There was one section on the east side near Hemme Avenue known then as "Judge's Row." There, several superior court judges of Alameda County came out via Hayward or Fish Ranch Road for the drive and eventually bought property.

One such was Judge Fred V. Wood* of Piedmont, whose wife was Laura May* (Ivory) Wood, a school teacher and granddaughter of pioneer David Glass. The Woods were married June 18, 1893. Her mother was Clara Isadora (Glass) Ivory, who married Edgar Durkee Ivory, brother to Marco Ivory, sheriff of Contra Costa County from 1871 to 1875.

Portions of a deed from the Bank of Martinez to Fred V. Wood, dated October 31, 1901 and recorded February 19, 1902, in Volume 92 of Deeds, at page 476, show 4.25 acres of land, more or less, being a portion of the "Original Ford Tract" in Rancho San Ramon. Fred V. and Laura Wood and their son Melvin V. Wood lived in Alamo from 1902 to December 1908. The property was called "Cabana Rosa" or "Rosewood." This was because

44

every variety of rose was planted there, along with many fruits and berries.

Lloyd E. Ivory married Kathryn Huber* January 23, 1909 in San Rafael. They and their family of six children lived in the house for about twenty-four years. The three youngest children were born in Alamo. While the Ivory family lived in the Alamo house, Fred V. Wood built a cabin for his family across from the old house in the early 1920s.

On October 1, 1937, Melvin V. Wood, son of Fred V. Wood, deeded the property to his wife, Genevieve S. Wood, and their son, Curtis S. Wood, born January 10, 1929, as joint tenants. And the ownership of the property so remains.

In a letter from Clara Isadora (Glass) Ivory, daughter of David and Eliza Jane (Hall) Glass, written from Martinez, May 8, 1908, to her brother Clement Rolla Glass, La Paz, Bolivia, she mentions: " . . . Fred Wood built himself, at odd times, seven rooms, bath and pantry. They have three rigs and two horses and everything to be comfortable. Fred still has his law office in Oakland . . . home Saturday and Sunday and most of the time Wednesday."

She further mentions: "I have bought five acres of fruit land at Alamo, all in bearing trees, pears, Royal Ann cherries and Muir peaches. Hope it will bring in an income. It is part of the Reis orchard which is being sold off in five and ten acre tracts. I am within a stone's throw of the station and about as far again from Laura's [her daughter] house. Dozens of Oakland and San Francisco people are investing in summer homes instead of camping, and all people with money are building nice bungalows. I shall build a little four-room bungalow with bath, pantry, front and back piazzas. I have a contractor figuring on it now. I had the well bored and will put up a windmill. The bungalow should be finished by the time you get here around Christmas." (He was murdered January 1, 1909 in Bolivia by bandits.)

Some of the trees that still grow in abundance in the area were called "tree of Heaven" and were also known as Alantis trees. They make a good stand and quickly multiply by root runners. Part of the property for a time was a cherry orchard.

And not too far away at 1234 Danville Boulevard, Alamo, was the property of Superior Judge Lincoln Church. A home was built there, but his wife did not want to move that far out to the country. The house was sold to the Eel family and then to Captain S. A. and Mrs. Matilda "Tillie" Jonker, who moved in in 1946. In 1963 they moved to Walnut Creek, where she remains. He died in 1982. Current residents are Ben and Bernice Nemanic. Judge Church lived in a large two-story home at 1222 Danville Boulevard, Alamo. It was torn down in about 1981.

*Author's footnotes: Kathryn (Huber) Ivory was president of Alamo Women's Club from 1927 to 1929. Mrs. Ivory still makes her home in Walnut Creek.

Laura May died July 29, 1930. She was fifty-seven years old. Judge Wood died January 29, 1936. He was sixty-nine years old. Fifteen hundred mourners attended his funeral service.

SILVA HOUSE
1412 SILVA DALE, ALAMO

The Silva house.

The house at the end of Silva Dale was built in March of 1907 and was part of the Tom B. Jenkins Ranch. Dr. Samuel J. Silva, a dentist from Oakland, bought the old farmhouse and ten acres from Miss Kate Henry of Alamo, on January 30, 1918. The wooden house is on the east part of the property adjacent to the San Ramon Creek. Dr. Silva also bought sixty-nine acres of hill land across the creek, where he built a barn. The barn is still standing and can be seen from the freeway at Livorna Road, Alamo.

The old farmhouse was remodelled in 1936 using the most modern items of the day. It is a two-story wooden house with a twenty- by forty-foot living room, which at one time was the entire old farmhouse. Dr. Silva and his wife Bess and their three children came out from Oakland every

The milkhouse and old barn off Livorna Road.

weekend to enjoy the ranch. Bess and her son Louis planted many trees purchased from Niles Nursery and transported by their auto. A variety of redwoods, elms, eastern maples, linden and sycamore trees, now over seventy-five feet tall, were planted in 1918 and 1919.

There is also a four-room guest cottage on the property. It has stained glass windows and old-fashioned light fixtures. It was used by Bay Area friends visiting in the country on weekends. The Silvas entertained extensively during the 1930s and 1940s. Dr. Samuel Silva passed away in October of 1946 and his wife in 1956. She left the property to her son, Louis Jackson Silva, also a dentist in Oakland.

Dr. Silva had a busy practice so rented the house to various families for several years. In 1962 a daughter, Laura A. Miller, married and lived in the house for four years while her husband Jim attended college. A son, Scott Louis, was born in the house and he still lives there, the fourth generation Silva to live in the house.

Originally with the house were ten acres of walnut and prune orchard. On June 20, 1955, Louis Silva sold the first of six lots to Donald R. and Audrey Senior. The second lot was sold to Umberto Cavallo in 1955, and later that same year Wesley Bailey of Pleasant Hill bought two lots. The Silva house is now on one acre.

Dr. Louis Silva and his wife Hazel held many parties at the old house in the 1960s and 1970s, for their city friends on weekends. They have been coming out to the house for nearly fifty years, to enjoy the country. Dr. Silva passed away on November 27, 1982. His widow lives in Oakland, in her home of forty years. Dr. Silva was active in E Clampus Vitus, Conference of California Historical Societies and other organizations. His widow Hazel was regional vice-president for Alameda and Contra Costa counties for the Conference of California Historical Societies and Alameda County Dental Society.

Laura A. Miller, their daughter, the third generation of Silvas to own the old house, received it from her father on January 30, 1981, exactly sixty-three years to the day that it was originally bought by her grandfather, Dr. Samuel Silva. She and her two sons, Scott Louis and Todd Edward, have lived in the house since August 1981 and remain as current residents. She is a member of the board of directors of the San Ramon Valley Historical Society and enjoys genealogy and astrology research.

CHANEY HOUSE
1432 CHANEY ROAD, ALAMO

This two-story house sitting up on its knoll was occupied by the Chaney family, for whom a street was named. Research has not pinpointed the date the house was built, but some information might indicated that it was built in the late 1870s. The colonial structure was said to have been built by Daniel Robert McPherson. At some time in history it was the home of Wally B. and Effa "Effie" Mae Goold.* She was the daughter of Daniel Robert and Rhoda McPherson, pioneer settlers of the San Ramon Valley. The original farm was about 640 acres, used for dairy and beef cattle, which was their source of income. "Effie" was well-known for her prize harness horses.

In checking old deeds, one recorded June 25, 1925 in Volume 491 Deeds, page 491, we note says "between the lands formerly owned by Effa Mae Goold and Fannie F. Twitchell, originally eight acres*, to Frank W. and Lillian Byrn Pope."

February 4, 1928 was the date of a deed from Lenore E. Chaney to B. J. Morris and his wife Della P. The house was then surrounded by seven acres. The Reverend Morris and his wife apparently never lived there. His church was in Quincy. He sold the front piece to Jesse Near, and at one

46

The Chaney house at 1432 Chaney Road in Alamo.

time the Alamo Lodge of A.M. & F.M. was planning to build its temple there. The property is a portion of the Rancho San Ramon near the San Ramon Creek.

It was built with very high ceilings, parlors, large entry and halls, but with only two small closets and a rather small unworkable kitchen. The house was rented out over the years and became run down. It is said that at one time the Harold Soders of Walnut Creek lived there and that he was a carpenter. A Nesbitt of radio fame who had a popular radio show was also a resident, according to some of the natives.

In March of 1947 Max and Virginia Meier rented the home and, with their three children, Trudy, Barbara and Richard, moved in. The children chose to go to the Walnut Creek schools because the bus pickup was very convenient. While they have lived there they have had several addresses, from rural routes in Walnut Creek to the present Alamo home delivery. On May 14, 1952 the Meiers bought the house and 3.7 acres from the Reverend

Morris. They lowered some ceilings, changed windows, remodelled and updated the kitchen, converted the front parlor into a bedroom and the entry hall into the dining room, and added closets. They are the current residents. Their three children still live in the general area. Trudy is near Sacramento, Barbara lives in Pleasant Hill, and Richard is in Walnut Creek. Mr. Meier is retired and still enjoys gardening. There are several lovely areas with some unusual plants and trees not often used in the San Ramon Valley. He trades by mail with an eastern nursery.

One out building was possibly an old granary, later used as a garage, which had to be moved due to the creek's flooding.

*Author's footnotes: Wally B. and Effa "Effie" Mae Goold—Information received from Wanda (Goold) Deardorff of Hickman, California, August 1983, who as a child visited this house with her parents, Charles Gardner and Allie (Johnson) Goold. Walter Bradley Goold was Charles G. Goold's youngest brother, and his wife Effa "Effie" Mae (McPherson) was a sister to

Mary (McPherson) Podva, who was Roger Podva's mother. The Walter B. Goolds had two children who were raised in this house, Gladys (Goold) Caffee and Gardner Goold.

Eight acres—Apparently one acre more or less was lost from the flooding of the creek and erosion.

On July 20, 1983, I visited this over-100-year-old home and walked through the garden areas and enjoyed chatting with the Meiers. Max plants in containers because of the pesky gophers!

"SEQUOIA GRANDE"
211 La Colina Drive, Alamo

The two-story Crozer home on La Colina Drive, off Las Trampas Road, Alamo, was built in 1913 for Enoch L. and Georgie Crozer of Alameda. Edward Sims, who studied under Bernard Maybeck of Berkeley, was the builder. The Crozers ran the Sunday School held in the Alamo Grammar School until Mrs. Crozer's death in 1928. Mr. Crozer passed away in 1936.

Their daughter Ruth continued to dwell in the house and married Max Giddings of Berkeley. She was a vocational nurse at Alta Bates Hospital in Berkeley. He worked at the toll gate at Mount Diablo entrance for a time. They named the home "Sequoia Grande" for a tree that was on the property* and lived there into their eighties. Ruth died in October 1975 and Max in 1976.

In June 1976 the home and one and one-half acres were sold in an estate sale to Mr. and Mrs. Arthur N. (Merrill) Beebe, Jr. of Alamo. They saved the basic structure and remodelled and restored it to its original state, using the old house plans and making additions as needed. Their contractor was Arnold Wexler of Oakland. They sold a half acre to her aunt and uncle, Mr. and Mrs. Richard (Alice) Walsh of Saratoga, who built a new home there.* The Beebes moved to Pennsylvania in 1980, where they bought a large mansion to restore. The house in Alamo was sold to Dr. and Mrs. John A. Crockett and their five children in September 1980. He is a physician. The Crocketts have added a wrought iron fence with gate entry.

*Author's footnote: When checking with Dr. Crockett I was told the large redwood is still there. I later drove over and saw it for myself!

Another half acre was sold to Bob and Janice Hess, who also built their home there.

COLONEL WHITE HOME
253 LARK LANE, ALAMO

A large three-story home on the hillside of the Las Trampas range was built sometime before the turn of the century by a Mr. Benson, who owned hundreds of acres around it. He was a very large man and surveyed his acreage from a cart drawn by two large horses. For many years the paths that were made by his much-traveled cart were visible to hikers when they walked the Las Trampas range. In addition to the big house there were a smaller house just below, two barns, away and detached from the house, and other necessary out buildings of the day, and those that struck his fancy! Each floor of the house opened out to beautiful terraced gardens. From the dining room one went out around a circular fishpond to a path that led around the hill to a formal toilet, with sections for men and women. Because of Benson's proportions, it is believed, the fountain outside the lower story was used for his personal bath. It was made of brick with a small iron railing set in the brick.

John Louis Morss and his wife Isabelle Christina (Flood) were married September 12, 1900, and with their daughter Ramona Loubelle* moved into the home following the San Francisco earthquake in 1906. The large house was in "apple pie order", it was said. The house was heated with fireplace heat on each floor, with one chimney for all. The kitchen stove furnished hot water. In 1912 a son Flood was born in the house. Loubelle passed away April 10, 1981 at Palm Springs at the age of seventy-nine.

The Colonel White home when the Morss family was living there, about 1912.

Above and below, two views of the Colonel White house, both taken in September 1983.

In 1913 Colonel William Lincoln White and his wife Inga became owners and remodelled and installed inside plumbing. Colonel White also renamed North Avenue to Las Trampas Road, saying it was more appropriate. He started the *Walnut Creek Courier Journal* on June 1, 1911. It later became the *Courier Journal* and still later the *Contra Costa Times*, which is now a daily "metrotype" newspaper.

In the early 1920s the Whites moved to New York for a time and rented to Captain Meyers and his wife, who was a Dunfee. After the Whites returned and the colonel passed away, in time his widow married Edward T. Lesure. Her husband was a bridge contractor and was known as "Ned." Mrs. Lesure was the owner of the house for about forty-two years.

About 1955 Mrs. Lesure sold to Phillip Fay of Alamo, and he rented out the big, old house and some horse pasture land. In 1974, an attorney, William D. McCann, and his wife Barbara and children purchased the old three-story house and its surrounding acreage and named it "Hide Park." The house had been badly abused and vandalized and they had it restored and remodelled and moved in in 1976. Their contractor estimated that the building had been restored at least seven times, and added to, as well. Two architects experienced in the art of Victorian reconstruction noted that the exterior portico on the west side might have been constructed in about 1890. The portico is rococo in nature, with plaster castings underneath the supports and on the Corinthian mantle above the western door of the house. The portico was added after the original structure was built. Nails removed from the second story veranda were hand-forged and typical of nails used in California residences constructed in the mid-nineteenth century.

In February 1980, Randy and Jan Nahas and their three children bought the house with five acres. Randy is a developer who specializes in restoration. He has several to his credit. They will continue restoring and redecorating the lovely old home, of which no one really seems to know the true age or can for sure authenticate its varied styling. They intend to be busy for some time.

*Author's footnote: Ramona Loubelle, named for San Ramon, where she was born, and Loubelle for her parents, Louis and Isabelle.

In mid-August 1983, all power poles were removed and utilities laid underground to enhance the beauty of this home and its grounds.

"RANCHO-ROMERO"
JONES RANCH
146 ROMERO CIRCLE, ALAMO

This two-story home has been in the Jones family since it was built in 1919.* Its housewarming was celebrated in October of that year. The builder was Fred Burnett of Alamo, who also built the Humburg/Jackson home on the knoll, the original site of the first Alamo postoffice* of 1852.

The interior of this home has lovely southern gum wood. All rooms are large with lots of storage closets. Several bedrooms are on the second floor. The master bedroom on the ground floor has a small nursery room adjoining, living room, dining room, den, kitchen with pantry room and breakfast room, large entry hall and screened-in back porch. Both floors have wide central hallways. There is a basement and there are three sets of interior stairways. There is a large covered porch on the south and east sections of the house—verandas, as they were known. In its "heyday" several gardeners kept up the grounds, and for years there was always a cook.

The house was built for James Cass Jones* and his wife Flora May (Stone) Jones*, who had one son Alden Albert Jones, born March 19, 1904, and a foster son, Alfred Bensen Jones*, born October 24, 1913, died December 20, 1980.

James Cass Jones was the son of pioneer John M.* and Mary Ann (Smith) Jones*, born in Alamo. On September 12, 1900 he married Flora May (Stone), born May 1, 1863 in Alamo. He died December 4, 1934, and she September 4, 1942.

Alden Albert Jones* married Josephine (Fowler*) Jones of Vacaville, California, June 14, 1931, in Alamo, and in 1942 they inherited the property. They had a daughter Marilyn Kay Jones, born May 12, 1937, and a son Gregory Alden Jones, born March 25, 1941. All attended local schools and graduated from San Ramon Valley High School. Current owner residents are the Alden A. Joneses. Following his graduation from the University of California at Davis, Alden Jones became a farmer and he was a farmer until his retirement.

Part of this ranch was subdivided in 1960 with two units, with the Joneses as grantors, William F.

Rancho-Romero in the early 1920s when the acreage was in vineyards, before it was walnut orchard. This photo shows the south side and the front of the house, which faces Mount Diablo.

This northeast view of the house at Rancho-Romero was taken about 1936. The house was built in 1919.

Anderson of Alamo as realtor, and John Osmundson, also of Alamo, as builder. The large front piece became Alamo Market Plaza Shopping Center and held its grand opening November 29 and 30 and December 1, 1956. Today it is the Alamo Plaza.

*Author's footnotes: This home was built in 1919, after the November 10, 1866 home at "Rancho-Romero" burned.

Alamo postoffice—now Alamo Village Shopping Center.

John M. Jones was the first postmaster, served nine and one-half years.

John M., Mary Ann, James C., Flora May, Alfred B. and baby Virginia Jones are all at rest in the old Alamo Cemetery. Alden A. Jones passed away September 17, 1983 at seventy-nine and one-half years.

During the mid-forties, the war years following Pearl Harbor, the Joneses opened their home to three couples from Georgia. The men were in the United States Navy, stationed at Camp Parks. They were: O. H. "Reid" and Dot Reid and their son Billy; Jimmie and Dorcas Hix; and Bill and Carolyn Butler. Correspondence is still carried on with some of them.

Fowler—Josephine's father was Herbert Franklin Fowler, born in San Francisco in August 1881. He died of pneumonia in 1922. Her mother was Josephine (Walworth) Fowler, born in Grass Valley in November 1877. She also died of pneumonia in 1922, during her husband's funeral. These were the days before antibiotics. Her brothers all worked in the Empire mine in

Nevada City. Herbert F. Fowler was a bookkeeper, and she worked in a bank also. They met in San Francisco when she came to attend business college. They enjoyed bicycling together during their courtship.

GRANDMA HUMBURG'S HOUSE
3990 DANVILLE BOULEVARD, ALAMO

In the Alamo downtown area there are two homes we know as the Humburg houses. Friederick Lorenz Humburg, born March 5, 1824 in Kassell, Germany, was married June 21, 1863 to Maria Kornmann, born April 16, 1837 in Zell-Romrod, Germany. They were married at the home of her sister, Mrs. Hoffman, in Alamo. He died June 30, 1886 and she in February 1918, both in Alamo. They are laid to rest in the Humburg Plot of the old Alamo Cemetery. This home was built for them and their family.

The one-story five-room house with huge attic and twelve-foot-high ceilings is a Victorian. It has a redwood foundation with pier boxes. There is also a well and pump and a barn on the property.

In 1939, Mrs. Friederiche (Humburg) Jackson sold this house to Ted (dec.) and Jerry* McIntyre. The McIntyres sold to Rex Mattson* in January 1973. His parents, "Sandy" and Moselle Mattson, and son Rex and daughter Suzanne, moved into the house in late 1972, a very cold winter. Rex Mattson is still the owner and the house is currently rented to Curtis and Nancy Reed, who moved in on May 16, 1982 from Lafayette, where they lived for two years after moving up from Orange County. They have a daughter Jennifer Nicole*, born April 15, 1983. Curtis is an electrician and commutes daily to San Francisco. They adore the old house and its grounds and hope to purchase it and remain forever.

*Author's footnotes: Jerry McIntyre makes her home in Roseburg, Oregon.

Rex mattson and his mother Moselle moved to Folsom, California, January 15, 1983 and are building a new home there. I interviewed Rex in May 1983.

Jennifer Nicole is the author's granddaughter's name, too.

It has been said that this old home was built before early tax records were kept and also that is was a stagecoach stop. Also, that one of the renters years ago apparently engaged in making "moonshine" in the house.

I visited this charming, quaint home in August 1983 and found it to be in very good shape and well cared for with nice large airy rooms and pleasant quiet enclosed garden areas with nice well kept lawn areas.

Grandma Humburg's house, August 1983. (Photo by Nancy Reed)

HUMBURG HOUSE NUMBER TWO
24 ORCHARD COURT, ALAMO

The second home we refer to as a Humburg house is at 24 Orchard Court, Alamo. It was built for August Humburg, who was born February 1, 1870 in Alamo, and his bride Annie Alice Stone, born June 25, 1868 in Alamo. They were married August 30, 1893 in Alamo and built the three-story Queen Anne Victorian soon after they were married. It is of redwood and cedar lumber and had living areas on the upper levels to ward off flooding from the San Ramon Creek. Their children Friederiche Humburg, later Jackson, and Lorenz (Lawrence) Albert Humburg, were born in the house, Friederiche on December 6, 1894 and her brother on May 10, 1896. They were active in church and community affairs.

Later owner/residents were Michael and Elizabeth Coakley, who lived there with their eight children. Michael was the uncle of Judge Thomas I. Coakley. They came from Oakland because of the mother's health. Michael Coakley* and his brother were in the meat business in Oakland. The sons and cousins delivered meat to Alameda County.

"Uncle Homer" and "Aunt Rene" Fuller followed, and they were favorites of the Jackson and Humburg children, who visited often. Charles Clark bought the house from the Fullers. The owners who followed the Clarks lowered the house and made rooms out of the upper portion, put in a new foundation, and rewired and replumbed the house.

In 1965 Phillip Fay, Jr. and his wife Nancy (Morison), daughter of Bill and Virginia Morison of Alamo, bought the house. They moved in with a daughter Lauren and a son Phillip III. A second son Patrick was born there. They lived there for eight years, until they moved to their present home on Vernal Drive, Alamo. They sold the old home to his father, Phillip John Fay, Sr. of Alamo, who rented it out. It became very rundown during this rental period.

In 1976 Fay sold to John C. Conrad and his wife Barbara and their three children, Stacey, Dana and Douglas.* The four-bedroom house, with two baths, living room, family room and kitchen, has been spruced up with redecorating to preserve its historic flavor. A partition of two small rooms was removed and extended out the rear, making a larger room. John C. Conrad works for Compass Container Company and commutes to Oakland. Barbara is a teacher at Stone Valley School in Alamo. Stacey lives in Pleasant Hill and Dana

53

A 1982 sketch of the August Humburg house, by Chris Arnott of the Valley Pioneer.

attends college. Douglas entered Monte Vista High School in the fall of 1983. The Conrads continue to restore and preserve and hope to live in the ninety-year-old home for a very long time. The two large magnolia trees still waft and share their perfume with the populace as in days gone by. For many years this home was used for local elections.

*Author's footnotes: Coakley—thanks to "Adobe Trails," publication of Hayward Area Historical Society, Vol. XV, No. 1, Spring 1978, for some information.

Douglas has a collection of beer cans from 1935 when the can was introduced for this product. He has 500, many of them the early types. This has given him an introduction to nostalgia, which hits many of us during our lifetimes. And thank goodness for that!

ALBERT WARD STONE HOUSE
140 AUSTIN LANE, ALAMO

The house later referred to as Commander Austin's house was built very close to the site of the original adobe of Jose Miguel Garcia and his wife Rafaela Miranda. This adobe was built in 1848. On December 4, 1855, the adobe and surrounding property were sold to William Comstock. In 1858 he sold these holdings to Colonel Albert Ward Stone and his wife Martha.

Colonel Albert Ward Stone and his wife Martha and son Edward Albert took the Overland Trail to California in 1853 and settled in Colusa. (He had

made the trip in 1852 as well.) In 1858 they came to Alamo and bought 400 acres adjoining his father Squire Silas Stone, who had settled there in 1853. The elder Stone was known as the alcalde in the district.

Later Albert Ward Stone purchased 800 more acres and continued to enlarge his property. It is said that, combined, the Stone properties went from what is now Stone Valley Road to Livorna Road. This vast portion of Alamo became known as Stone Valley, and several members of this family had their homes and farms there.

The 1848 Garcia adobe consisted of five rooms, with porches front and back. Albert Stone added a frame building of three rooms on the north end, making a comfortable eight-room house for his family. The four younger Stone children were born in this pioneer home. They were: Alonzo Lincoln, July 29, 1860, died January 10, 1928; Flora May, May 1, 1863, died September 4, 1942; Susie, May 10, 1866, died September 1, 1904; and Annie Alice, June 25, 1868, died July 19, 1939. All were born and died in Alamo.

Improvements began at once: barns, granary*, poultry houses, shops, fences and corrals and orchards and vineyards. The old Spanish ranch became a place of industry and progress!

In the 1860s Albert Stone planned to build a fine concrete house on the site of the old adobe. (It was before the days of reinforced concrete.) When the

Mrs. Annie Humburg and her children Friederiche and Lorenz in the front yard at 24 Orchard Court. Photo circa 1897.

1868 earthquake destroyed concrete warehouses in Pacheco, he gave up the idea. The old adobe, however, withstood the shock well, with only a few cracks.

About 1869 Stone built a large frame house of twelve rooms, on high ground, north of the original adobe. About 1870 a windmill* and tank were erected. And in the 1880s a fine spring of water in the hills on the southeast part of the ranch was piped to a reservoir built in an excavation at the top of the "vineyard hill." It was about a quarter mile north of the house. The reservoir was built of brick, jug-shaped and lined with cement. It had a capacity of 100,000 gallons and supplied the house, gardens, barns and many troughs with an abundance of water. (It still exists on the property of the John Lasagna family* at 211 Austin Lane, unchanged and currently used for storage.) Albert Ward Stone died August 27, 1890 in his Alamo home.

This Stone home was deeded to his daughter Martha Jeannette (Stone) and her husband Edward Augustus Bunce, November 5, 1891. Bunce died March 18, 1908, and the property remained his widow's until 1935, when she sold it to Commander Frank Austin and his wife Lenore. She always intended to name the street Bunce Meadows Lane, but the Pacific Gas and Electric Company named it Austin Lane, as Austin was then living in the big old house. So she gave that name to the street off Miranda Avenue where the old granary was and a part of the original Stone Ranch.

Austin built a smaller home on the site of the adobe for his family use and sold the big frame house in 1958-59 to Jack and Ann MacMillan. (Jack was a nephew of Olivette (Bunce) McMillan (dec.).)

*Author's footnotes: Granary and windmill are still existing and in operation at Bunce Meadow Lane.

John and Tina Lasagna bought the three-acre piece with the reservoir and a small cottage in early 1950. They built a new home for their family use in 1960. The vineyard is still on the property.

John Lasagna owns and operates West Brae Nursery Garden Supply at 1272 Gilman Street in Berkeley. My parents lived in Albany, where I was raised, and we were customers for years. Their daughter Michele teaches fifth grade at Rancho-Romero School in Alamo. She co-authored a book on California Indians with another local school teacher, Gail Faber of Danville. It has recently been approved as a supplement in the California school system. They are busy writing their second book on California's missions.

William Stone standing beside the house at 140 Austin Lane, Alamo, north of the former site of the Garcia adobe.

BUNCE MEADOW HOUSE
(PART OF ALBERT WARD STONE RANCH)
100 BUNCE MEADOW DRIVE, ALAMO

The two-story granary was built about 1858 and was part of the Albert Ward Stone Ranch. It was remodelled and a large addition was built by Kjell and Martha (Bunce) Johnsen during the early 1920s, when they returned from Orick, California to live in Alamo.

Bunce Meadow house.

In July 1964 it was sold to the Edward L. Pope family, who in June 1966 sold to Ronald E. and Jerry Kirkham. Off and on, for a time—it is said—there were other tenants. The Kirkhams sold to Ronald and Dorothy Kelleher in July 1975. In November 1975 the Kellehers and Anthony Perez sold the house with one acre to Emmett and Sharon Doherty, Jr. They and their two children, a daughter Erin, born July 1967, and a son Dan, born October 1968, continue to live there and improve, redecorate and restore.

They completely rewired the house, added a fireplace, sanded, painted and wallpapered every room in an early country decor; redid all landscaping, saving only the picket fence, native garden and rocks from the original property, resurfaced an old pond and landscaped around it, replaced the old barbed wire fencing with wooden fence, improved the small barn and ring and created a pasture for horses. The original 1870 windmill was reactivated and now operates on wind power.

The Doherty family continue to tend the property, keeping it to its original flavor, raising chick-ens, pets of cats, dogs and horses. They found two boards inscribed by Silas Stone and one by E. L. (Elwin Lucius) Stone, which they treasure as keepsakes. They feel it is a wonderful place to work, live and play. Their sign out fronts reads "The Farmhouse"—its new name.

*Author's footnote: See Albert Ward Stone House for further details.

BENNETT HOUSE
1403 CASA VALLECITA, ALAMO

The property of the Mannings, for whom a street was named, was eleven acres on the east side of Danville Boulevard, Alamo. It later was named Casa Vallecita. The Bennett family moved from Santa Cruz because of its fog, and bought the property, which had some walnut trees on it. Builder Fred Burnett of Walnut Creek, and later Alamo, built the house in the middle of the eleven acres, in 1919. Its address was 2840 Danville Boulevard. It was a two-story house with eleven rooms and a furnace which first used coal, then oil, and later was converted to gas. There are water wells plus pump and tool houses on the property. Mr. Bennett was a retired farmer from Iowa. He planted prune trees in the front and walnut trees in the rear, plus a family fruit orchard. The house had lovely interior wood and still has washbasins in the closets.

Longtime residents of Alamo remember Mr. Bennett as having one of the first automobiles in the area—and watching it speed past. It has been said that he was an avid fisherman but didn't like to eat fish, so he gave them away, always with scales and just as caught. The Bennetts held many church parties in their home.

In 1940 Ewell W. Slade and his wife Michaela bought the property from Alamo realtor Edward G. Fagan. They dug more wells with very good water. The property included the house with five acres in back, and they later bought the front five acres as well. The Slade family moved in with their daughter Barbara and son Robert, who had both been born in Kobe, Japan, as had their father. When Mr. Slade was twelve he was sent to the United States to continue his education.

Mr. Slade was an import export merchant, for thirty years in Japan and later in California, with Asian ports including Vietnam. The Slades were married in 1929. Both of their children attended local schools and graduated from San Ramon Valley High School. They are school teachers. E. W. Slade passed away in 1980.

In 1952 the prune trees were torn out as their market was no longer profitable and the taxes were going up. The Slades subdivided the front section, with Carl Hansen as builder of the speculative homes. Carl's wife Juanita named the street Casa Vallecita. The old house had a change of address to 1403 Casa Vallecita.

In 1977 builder Vern Ryan and his wife Gladys[*] of Danville bought the old house and five acres from the Slades. They reinforced its foundation, renovated and redecorated and were going to make it their own home. They also laid underground utilities and built one speculative home which was sold to Fred Redmond. The five acres were subdivided into nine half-acre lots. The Slades moved into a home at 1409 Casa Vallecita, the former Carl Hansen home. Four other homes were built by different builders.

In 1978 the 1919 house was sold to Tim Beem, son of well-known photographer Ted Beem of Diablo. Tim and his wife and four children are the current owners. The house went on the market at the end of July 1983, for $285,000, as the Beems will be moving to Truckee, California. It sold in four days.

[*]Author's footnotes: Ewell W. Slade's family got their start in the gold rush days.

When the freeway came in 1965 the back acre was cut off from the rest of the street and the San Ramon Creek was diverted.

Vern and Gladys Ryan sold their Stone Valley Road home to Fred Redmond and they moved on Cross Road in Alamo Oaks, where they raise blue ribbon Arabian horses.

The Bennett house, built in 1919. (Photo courtesy of Tim Beem)

This sketch of the old Alamo Cemetery was made by Nan Soldahl. (Courtesy Alamo Plaza Merchants Association)

THE OLD ALAMO CEMETERY
END OF EL PORTAL ROAD, ALAMO

It seems fitting to finish this book on old homes and buildings in the San Ramon Valley by including a piece on the old Alamo Cemetery. Many of the early owners of San Ramon Valley buildings are now at rest there. The article was researched by the author as an appointed trustee of the Alamo-Lafayette Cemetery District in December 1982.

The old Alamo Cemetery site is at the end of El Portal Road off Danville Boulevard, the main street through the unincorporated town of Alamo, in Contra Costa County in northern California. This small public cemetery is situated on the south end of Alamo, on the cusp of the neighboring city of Danville.

It is a two and one-half acre site, perched on a rounded hill protected by majestic Mount Diablo to the east and the Las Trampas range to the west, with some rolling hills in between. It is a parklike setting with many lovely trees including stately old oaks and pines. At the top is a wooden arbor with benches for a rest spot.

The cemetery is of historic significance, and the San Ramon Valley Historical Society placed a bronze plaque at the entry gateway designating its one hundred twenty-fifth year, on May 31, 1980, with appropriate ceremonies which were attended by a good number of residents from the valley and surrounding areas.

Many pioneers and persons of historic significance are buried in this quaint old cemetery. Residents of Alamo, Danville, parts of San Ramon (all part of the San Ramon Valley) and neighboring cities of Walnut Creek and Lafayette are eligible to purchase burial plots. They must, however, be part of the cemetery district.

The cemetery is governed by the Board of Trustees* of the Alamo-Lafayette Cemetery District, which belongs to the California Association of Public Cemeteries. There are three trustees appointed to four-year terms by the Contra Costa County Supervisors.* They volunteer their time with no pay, and meet once a month. There is a paid superintendent* who takes care of all the records and necessary duties to be done, working out of an office building at the Lafayette Cemetery site.

The true age of the Alamo Cemetery is questionable. By some research it is said this cemetery had a burial of an Indian or Spaniard in 1801, and a burial of a member of an early survey party in 1838. However, the first official recorded date was 1856—a six-year-old girl whose parents lived in Danville. Her memorial marker still stands in the cemetery.

Tracing the back-chain of title to this cemetery

59

reveals that an agreement was executed July 1, 1865 and recorded November 13, 1865, in which Horace W. Carpentier agreed to convey his interest in the Rancho San Ramon to Golder Fields and others.

By patent dated April 7, 1866 and recorded July 22, 1867, legal title was confirmed to said Carpentier and to Rafaela Soto de Pacheco, Nicolas Pacheco, Ines Pacheco and Lorenzo Pacheco. By subsequent agreement dated July 1, 1865, recorded December 28, 1868, Golder Fields agreed to pay to Thomas A. Brown, trustee, certain monies necesary to purchase the interest of Carpentier in said rancho.

Legal title having been vested in trust, in execution and discharge, a deed dated May 30, 1870 and recorded June 4, 1870, conveyed to John P. Chrisman, J. J. Kerr, Orris Fales, R. B. Love, George McCamly and J. K. Lassing, as trustees of the Alamo Cemetery Association, and to their successors in office, all the land shown as the "2.24 acres" on the map of Rancho El Rio, filed March 24, 1910, in the Contra Costa County records, and also the land lying east of the San Ramon Creek, being executed from the deed to the Cumberland Presbyterian Church, built in 1856.

Also, in discharge of the trust, Thomas A. Brown, trustee, conveyed to R. B. Love, J. J. Kerr, Thomas Flournoy and John Baker, trustees of the Cumberland Presbyterian Church, the lands lying between Alamo Cemetery Association parcel and the Martinez and San Ramon Road. Said deed was dated May 30, 1870 and recorded June 4, 1870. Said cemetery association conveyed two fifty-foot strips to the County of Contra Costa (along the south line of the church parcel and the other along the east bank of San Ramon Creek), deeded and recorded December 9, 1908.

By a deed recorded July 21, 1937, E. B. Anderson, Charles Wood, Chester A. Love, Edward C. Wiester and Alden A. Jones, directors of the Alamo Cemetery Association, conveyed to the Alamo-Lafayette Cemetery District, a political subdivision of the State of California "that certain 2.24 acre tract and parcel designated and delineated on map of Rancho El Rio and subdivision of a portion of the Rancho San Ramon, records of Contra Costa County." By deed recorded June 14, 1944, Alamo-Lafayette Cemetery Association quitclaimed to Contra Costa County that portion aforementioned.

*Author's footnote: Board of trustees members are: Dorothy G. Mutnick, chairman, of Lafayette; Primo E. Facchini and Virgie V. Jones, both of Alamo.

Contra Costa County supervisors—District 1, Tom Powers; District 2, Nancy C. Fahden; District 3, Robert I. Schroder, current 1983 chairman; District 4, Sunne Wright McPeak; and District 5, Tom Torlakson.

The superintendent for the Alamo-Lafayette Cemetery District is Christine E. Schreiber of Lafayette.

This sketch of the old cemetery was made by Chris Arnott, Valley Pioneer.

Chapter Nine

Potpourri

Contra Costa County in northern California is so rich in history it would be remiss not to include other historical buildings not in the San Ramon Valley. Therefore, the author will include this courtesy chapter for historical buildings from *some* neighboring areas surrounding the San Ramon Valley—not all, or this would never get to the printers.

CONTRA COSTA COUNTY'S ADOBES

First, we must not forget to mention, with pride, the existing five adobes left in our county. They probably were the beginning of civilization, as we know it, in Contra Costa County, and it is wonderful to still have them to help remind us of the early history.

The oldest is the Don Jose Joaquin Moraga Adobe, built in 1841, overlooking the Moraga Valley and Saint Mary's College at a distance. Moraga's children and grandchildren lived there until 1885. The Nunes family lived there from 1903 to 1919. The old adobe was salvaged and restored in 1941, its one-hundredth year, by Mrs. James Irvine, who was born in 1886 and spent her retiring years in the adobe, where she died in 1950. She willed it to her twelve-year-old grandson. In 1964 it was purchased by Donald E. Manuel, who was the first president of the Moraga Historical Society. It is now the home of Dean Claxton.

The two adobes in Concord are the Don Fernando Pacheco Adobe, built in 1844, at 3119 Grant Street, and the Don Salvio Pacheco Adobe, which was completed June 24, 1854, at 2050 Adobe Street.

The two adobes in Martinez are the Vicente Martinez Adobe and the Altamirano Adobe. The Martinez Adobe is located on the grounds of the John Muir National Historic Site. It was built in 1849 by Vicente, who lived there until 1853, when he sold it to Edward Franklin, for whom Franklin Canyon was named. It became the home of Muir's daughter Wanda and her husband Thomas Hanna, in 1906. Muir often dined there with them.

The Altamirano Adobe on Alhambra Valley Road, Martinez, was built by Abelino, son of Luis Altamirano. By some references it is said to have been built as early as 1840. However, research says Abelino built it after he married Maria de la Encarnacion Martinez, born in 1808, and married after March 1850. In 1881 it was purchased by John F. Swett, founder of California's public school system. The Thomas L. Sharman family live there currently and the address is 295 Millthwait Drive.

*Author's footnote: My thanks to Thomas F. Gates, County Library at Pleasant Hill, and Brother Dennis, Saint Mary's College Library, for information and updating.

EARLY GOVERNMENT

A true history buff author repeats history to refresh the reader's interest. California's history can be divided into five distinct eras: Indian occupation, Spanish exploration, mission and settlement days, the Mexican or rancho period, and, after 1850, statehood.

Contra Costa County's beginning was part of California's history before the state became a state in 1850. As early as February 26, 1839, California was to receive its first colonized government. There were three districts, with Contra Costa County part of the second. All districts were under the jurisdiction of Governor Juan Bautista Alvarado and a departmental assembly, holding sessions at the then capital at Monterey. Under the governor were the prefects in charge of districts, sub-prefects, and on a local level, town councils and alcaldes, followed by the justices of the peace.

It was planned to have a Superior Tribunal, to be divided among courts to be titled First Instance and so on. Courts of the First Instance were to be located in the chief towns of the districts. These would involve cases over $100. The lesser sums came under the local rule. Here we learn that the alcalde's word was supreme in legal matters of that time. Though this early form of government was simplistic, the plan never fully materialized.

In 1849, California was governed by a constitution passed by the territorial government. Contra Costa County, of which Alameda County was then a part, was a part of the San Jose District, where the first constitution was formed. San Jose was the state's capital. On September 1, 1849, the convention met at Monterey, where Benicia's Robert Semple, a delegate from the District of Sonoma, was chosen president. The session lasted six weeks.

The first legislature of California convened at San Jose on December 15, 1849, when the state had twenty-seven counties. The Honorable Elam Brown of La Fayette was a member of the convention to form a constitution, passed by the territorial government. General Mariano Guadalupe Vallejo was a member of the first legislature. The current California constitution, which has been amended many times, was adopted in 1879.

Until 1845 the white population of California numbered about five thousand people. Mainly they were Spanish and Mexican cattle raisers called rancheros, and priests and soldiers. Also there were a few American and northern European traders, trappers and pioneers. By 1849, the population had risen to more than 92,000, because of the gold hopefuls. By 1860, California's population was 380,000 people, most of them having come from the eastern states. Also thousands of Chinese coolies were imported during this time, to help build the railroads. In 1869, when the first trans-continental railroad was completed, large numbers of pioneers continued to come from the east coast states.

The land boom of the 1880s brought midwesterners. California's population grew by 65.7 percent between 1920 and 1930, more than any other state—and it continues, doubling its population each twenty years.

STATE SYMBOLS

The state seal features the Golden Gate with the Sierra Nevada as a background. Minerva, goddess of wisdom, is at the right side. On top is the state motto, "Eureka," meaning "I have found it." The state flag is a brown bear in the center of a white field, with "California Republic" beneath the bear. There is a red star in the upper left corner and a red band at the bottom. This state flag was adopted February 3, 1911. The Americans revolted against Mexican rule on June 14, 1846 at Sonoma.

In 1931 the state bird became the California valley quail (*Laphortyx californica*). In 1903 the golden poppy (*Eschscholtzia californica*) was adopted. Many used to grow along the roadways. The California grizzly bear is the state animal, and the California golden trout the state fish. The California redwood is its tree. "I Love You California" is the state song, and the state is known as "the golden state."

CALIFORNIA'S SEVEN FLAGS*

Flags flying over California were: Spanish for 280 years, from 1542 to 1822; English for thirty-seven days only, planted by Sir Francis Drake, who named California New Albion; Russian for thirty years, from 1811 to 1841 at a colony near Bodega Bay. In 1822 the flag of the Mexican Empire flew for only a few months. The flag was that of the Republic of Mexico from 1823 to 1846 and the Republic of California from June 14, 1846 to July 7, 1846 (the bear flag), followed by the flag of the United States of America.

And now—back to the buildings and old homes.

*Author's footnote: Some of the information about California's seven flags came from the California State Library in Sacramento via Abbie Dopp of Walnut Creek, California History and Landmarks Chairman of California Federation of Women's Clubs, 1981-82.

Shadelands Ranch Historical Museum.

SHADELANDS RANCH HOUSE
2660 YGNACIO VALLEY ROAD
WALNUT CREEK

It was in 1853 that Hiram Paul Penniman* purchased part of an original Mexican land grant from the pioneer Pacheco family. His wife was Carrie Gardiner Morris of Oakland and they had a daughter Bessie. The home was built in 1902 and they moved in in March of 1903.

Later it was owned by the Gospel Foundation of California, founded by Bessie's husband, Albert M. Johnson, and deeded to the city of Walnut Creek by them to be used as an historical museum. Edmund Moyer was hired as ranch manager in 1921 and served until his death in 1943. His son Gordon took over until 1950, when he moved to Tahoe. His wife was Marion Mayhew.

From 1952 to 1956 it was Shadelands School for the cerebral handicapped children. The school moved to larger quarters in Concord, keeping the name.

Shadelands Ranch Historical Museum is managed by the Walnut Creek Historical Society, which since 1971 has presented many productions to benefit Shadelands. These shows have contributed over $28,000 to the Walnut Creek Historical Society. The Shady Ladies, a group of volunteers, maintain it and sponsor the annual Tulip Tea Open House each April.

Beverly Clemson of Walnut Creek has been director since 1973. She has always strived for authenticity, which can be noted as one tours the building. Mannikins are dressed in authentic

gowns and featured in each room. Gaslight fixtures are in the living and dining rooms and one bedroom upstairs. The dining room is equipped with a fine collection of silver, china and glassware. There is a collection of *Atlantic Monthly* magazines from 1850 to 1863. The kitchen portrays what the turn-of-the-century housewife operated with in her daily chores.

In 1943 the downstairs front porch was enclosed to be utilized as a bedroom for the ranch manager's children. Later the museum made it into an exhibit room.

The history room upstairs contains much memorabilia and newspapers, including the *Walnut Kernel** weekly newspaper from 1932 to 1967, and 1,400 photographs, many books and maps.

Shadelands Ranch Historical Museum is open to the public every Wednesday and Sunday from 1:00 P.M. to 4:00 P.M. at no charge. In the spring of 1983, the board of directors was headed by the following officers: Robert Schroder, president; his wife Frances, vice-president; Ed McMunn, second vice-president; Anabell Martin, recording secretary; Katy Doherty, corresponding secretary; and Patricia Jadick, treasurer. There are fifteen other board members. The board voted to endorse a plan for the Shadelands Ranch Historical Museum to expand the use of its buildings and grounds, with vote results of thirteen to four. The plan is for the Walnut Creek Historical Society and Civic Arts to agree to do a designers showcase. This would refurbish and decorate the building that later could develop into a tea room or gift shop. This would allow Shadelands Ranch Historical Museum to be used for more functions with more participation. It is the plan to open the building six days a week. This plan has been controversial and nothing definite has been decided at this writing.

*Author's footnotes: Walnut Creek—How it got its name—Taken from the creek which the Spanish, in 1810, named "El Arroyo de los Nogales," meaning "the creek of the walnuts." About 1850 it was known as "the corners" with several explanations: as the junction between Oakland-Martinez-Livermore-Stockton, or the four Spanish land grants cornered there, or the crossroads for farmers, miners, tradesmen, stockmen and travelers in all directions.

Penniman—He was a civic leader and helped found the Contra Costa Agricultural Society in 1859. (Its first meeting was at Lafayette January 1, 1859, with Nathaniel Jones as president and Charles Bonnard secretary.) In 1865 he bought land in Walnut Creek proper, and changed the county road which had followed the creek (most roads did) and opened Main Street. He offered lots for sale, establishing the town of Walnut Creek. He also served on the county grand jury.

My thanks to Bev Clemson, who sent some information for my use.

Walnut Kernel newspaper—I was a by-lined columnist for this county-wide newspaper, writing about the San Ramon Valley, from May 28, 1953 to April 18, 1958.

PLEASANT HILL GRAMMAR SCHOOL
2050 OAK PARK BOULEVARD
PLEASANT HILL

This is the oldest public building in Pleasant Hill. The Pleasant Hill Grammar School on the 1.9 acres triangular piece of property is possibly the fourth or fifth grammar school for the area. It was under construction in 1918-19 and was completed in 1920, when it opened with an enrollment of about forty students.

The school was on the property of Edward A. Rodgers family, about a quarter mile from their farmhouse. Edward A. Rodgers was born in 1839 in Gorton, County Tyrone, Ireland and married Letitia Kinney, who was born in 1851 in Philadelphia, Pennsylvania. He died May 11, 1915 and she in 1920.

The student population grew from eleven pupils in 1912 to 220 in the 1940s. In 1949 the Pleasant Hill School District merged with several other small school systems and became the Mount Diablo Unified School District. From 1949 to 1959 the number of students increased from 220 to 6,425, in the Pleasant Hill area.

"My Recollections of Opening Day 1920" by eye witness Stanley Kramer, class of 1926, describes the school well. Through the front door was the combined principal's office of J. Ray Warne and a library lined with bookcases and books. The distinguished feature of the new school was its auditorium. It was used for school graduations and pageants and had a basketball court for intramural and interscholastic use. A space under the stage, at the north end, provided storage for folding chairs and wood necessary for the large woodburning stoves at the back of each of the two classrooms. Two lavatories at the south end of the building were properly labelled for gender. Also at the south end was a kitchen where the mothers of the P-TA prepared huge pots of potato soup to warm the children at lunchtime during the damp, cold winter months. There was a schoolyard for other games and stables for the students' saddle horses. On the west side of the school the students planted corn, pumpkins and melon vines, watered adequately from a well. Water was pumped from the shallow well by a one-cylinder gasoline engine and stored in the water tower above. From the front steps was a view of Mount Diablo, to be enjoyed in all seasons. The building was used as a school until 1950, when a new school close by was ready for occupancy.

Later a third classroom was added to its original two, and a Mr. Reilly and Mary Mendenhall were

Pleasant Hill Grammar School.

among the teachers. School principals were J. Ray Warne, 1920; Irene Spencer, 1927; Gladys Brown, 1946; and John Marshall, 1947. In 1920, while Mr. Warne was principal, his wife Helen was the teacher for grades one through four while he taught fifth through eighth.

In the early 1950s, the Pleasant Hill Recreation and Park District took over the old schoolhouse for recreational activities. From July 1970 to March 1981, when its new building was completed, the Pleasant Hill Police Department was there.

In the summer of 1979 a group of Pleasant Hill organizations formed a consortium to save the fine old building for a cultural-community center. In 1982 this consortium consisted of the Pleasant Hill Arts Council, Friends Abroad, Friends of the Pleasant Hill Central Library, Contra Costa Guild of Quilters, Pleasant Hill Historical Society, On-Stage Productions, and Veterans of Foreign Wars, and is now called the Pleasant Hill Historical and Cultural Center.

On March 26, 1983 the Mount Diablo Unified School District Board, by a vote of three to two, agreed to sell the old 1920 schoolhouse for $161,600 under a complicated agreement.

It became a mini-museum for the society and the Onstage Theatre*, with performances beginning June 26, 1982, even before it was completed. It was fully completed by March 1983 and held its second dedication ceremonies March 8, 1983. Twenty-five descendants of Edward A. Rodgers were present, including six-month-old baby Peter. The middle room of the Pleasant Hill Historical and Cultural Center was named in honor of Edward A. Rodgers.

How Pleasant Hill got its name—It is rumored that one brother said to another brother, "That's a pleasant hill," as they enjoyed the scenery.

* Author's footnotes: My thanks to Stanley Kramer of Pasadena, California, for his "Recollections of Opening Day 1920," and to Vallie Jo Whitfield and Henry F. and Ellie Greenfield of Pleasant Hill, for information for my use.

Onstage Theatre—I have seen several performances in this theatre and enjoyed them, especially the closing night of "George Washington Slept Here."

1983 current enrollments: Mount Diablo District, 31,828; Richmond, 27,710; and San Ramon Valley, the third largest of K-12 school districts in Contra Costa County, at 14,200 students.

BENJAMIN SHREVE STORE
3535 PLAZA WAY, LAFAYETTE

Benjamin Shreve, an eastern schoolteacher, crossed the plains in 1852, arriving in Lafayette in September of that year. He was born August 2, 1828 in Crawford County, Pennsylvania and was educated at Waterford Academy. He married Adaline Gorham, whose father was James H. Gorham. They had two sons, Fred and Milton. Benjamin Shreve taught school for two years in 1853-54. He then took over a roadside hotel-general store near Second Street and Golden Gate Way, and began his merchandise business. In the early 1860s he moved his business two blocks west.

In 1864 he built Benjamin Shreve's Store. Later it included the post office and an insurance agency. The family home was to its right. In 1857 Shreve petitioned Congress to establish a post office on his place, requesting the name of Centerville. Since one by that name was already established, he suggested La Fayette.* According to the National Archives at Washington, D.C., Shreve was appointed postmaster March 2, 1857 and served almost thirty years. His son Milton managed the store until it was sold to Henry A. Sweet.

In 1902 Robert Elam* McNeil, son of William and Jane (Allen) McNeil, and his wife Gertrude (Thomson), daughter of Robert and Charlotte (Maloney) Thomson, both born and raised in Lafayette, bought the store from Sweet's widow. When a boy Robert McNeil had worked for Shreve. The McNeils had five children: Chester Stuart, Ruth, Alice, William McKinley and Bertha. McNeil enlarged and remodelled the store and the sign read Robert E. McNeil, General Merchan-

The Handlebar, former Shreve Store which was built in 1864. This photo was taken in July 1983.

The Benjamin Shreve Store.

dise. He later changed the name to Pioneer Store. It was the gathering place for the local people. He put a false front on the building, though the back portion is the original to this day. Many forms of amusement were enjoyed, such as baseball, foot races, horseshoes and wrestling in the afternoons and evenings. The only telephone in town was in the store, and Alice McNeil and her brother William M. ran the messages for five cents. When the recipient was at some distance, like all the way to Sadie Moraga's in Moraga, William would ride his pony and receive twenty-five cents! R. E. McNeil did business with Theodore Russi at the Pacheco Mill, not knowing then that Theodore would marry his daughter Alice* and become his son-in-law.

R. E. McNeil, George Merideth and George Smith helped in the erection of the town hall in 1914. Gertrude McNeil and Margaret Rosenberg helped to establish perpetual care at the Lafayette Cemetery. McNeil passed away February 2, 1935, and his widow sold to George Hinckley and his sister, Ethel Emmert.

In 1941 it became a grocery store, the Market Basket, owned by a Mr. Cooper. In February 1942, Vincent J. Lombardo of Lafayette took over the meat department and in 1943 he bought the grocery store and called it Pioneer Food Store. His wife Sarah (Davi) stayed home and raised the family. They are natives of Pittsburg, California and currently residents of Lafayette.

At one time prior to the 1960s a Mrs. Waldie owned the building and it was known as Toyland. In December 1969, John Booth bought it from her son Scott and reopened it in January 1970. George Coupe of Alameda was a recent owner, while John Booth has operated the Handlebar, a bicycle and toy shop, as it currently remains. Early in 1983 the building was sold to Jack Monroe Trust of Lafayette.

*Author's footnotes: How Lafayette got its name— In research there is nothing to substantiate the long-time rumor that La Fayette was named after the Marquis de La Fayette, the French hero of the Revolution, an aide to George Washington. But the presumption exists and is often used in writings. We don't know if Benjamin Shreve was a student of history. We do know the La Fayette spelling was used for a long time in the history and existence of Lafayette, along with its present one-word spelling. It is more likely Lafayette was named from Shreve's wife's family members, the Gorhams, who came to California from Lafayette County, Wisconsin.

Robert Elam McNeil was named for Elam Brown, early pioneer and founder of Lafayette.

My thanks to Mrs. Alice McNeil Russi of Rossmoor for some of this information, and to Joan Merryman for her help at the Lafayette Library, where we met July 25, 1983.

Also to William L. McNeil, grandson of Robert E. McNeil and nephew of Mrs. Russi, for information taken from his "Some Reflections on the Pioneer Store 1855-1935," written June 20, 1963.

DE LAVEAGA MANSION "BIEN VENIDA" 12 BIEN VENIDA, ORINDA

Jose Vincente de Laveaga journeyed from Spain to Mexico where he was interested in silver mines and banking. From Mazatlan to Spain in 1857, he visited San Francisco, where he later became prominent in banking. One of his sons, Miguel, married Marie Le Breton, daughter of the Edward Le Bretons of San Francisco.

In September 1887 Miguel and Jose de Laveaga purchased 1,178.04 acres from Philip Barth for $50,880. They divided the property between them. In 1888 Miguel and his wife built a large, beautiful home on the hill above Miner Road in Orinda. They named it "Bien Venida," which loosely translates to "welcome." H. M. Waterbury was commissioned to build the road which became Bien Venida. This first home was taken by fire in 1915. It was immediately rebuilt in the same plan that same year. Out buildings of barns and other ranch buildings were included. The place was surrounded by lovely garden areas, arbors, lawn tennis court, a natural swimming pool and bathhouse.

A son of Miguel, Edward I. de Laveaga, born in 1884, was a lifetime resident. He was known as "E.I." He married Delight Woodbury, from a pioneer Oakland family, in 1906. They raised their children at Bien Venida. In 1921 "E.I." subdivided and built a small lake and put in six winding roads.

He named them Adrilla, El Toyonal, Canon Drive, Vallecito Lane, La Madronal and El Rincon. He called the lake Orinda, and Lake Orinda was also the name of his first subdivision.

A system of springs, wells, water pumps, tanks, valves, siphons, cut-offs and trails was developed to supply water for the new homes-to-be. He named the springs Fern, South Fork, Twin, Middle Fork, Quail, Toyonal, Coal, Rabbit and Current. All water was caught in Lake Orinda, which later became Orinda Park Pool.* By October 1922, one-third of the lots had been sold.

De Laveaga's plans for a village complete with all services were realized, plus later expansions including the Orinda Country Club in 1924. "E.I." de Laveaga died December 31, 1958, and his first wife Delight in 1960.

The de Laveaga family are responsible for much of the development of Orinda. The family home has been enjoyed by fourth and fifth generations. The de Laveagas have lived at Bien Venida since it was first built in 1915.

Edward L. "Ned" de Laveaga, grandson of Miguel the builder, and his wife Alysone (Hales) of Pasadena, have lived in the home since 1960. They raised their four children there, who had a wonderful growing up with fringe benefits of learning to be good gardeners! The three oldest children are married and there are five grandsons—enough for a basketball team. Family re-

"Bien Venida," de Laveaga mansion in Orinda, built in 1915.

unions are large and much fun, with activities including baseball, volleyball, badminton and croquet. It is the hope for this lovely old home with its history to stay in this family forever.

*Author's footnotes: How Orinda got its name—probably from the English poetess Katherine Fowler Philips, who was known as "Orinda" and so named in *Lives of the Poets*, Vol. 1.
Orinda Park Pool—In the 1940s I enjoyed much swimming there.

HACIENDA DE LAS FLORES
2100 DONALD DRIVE, MORAGA

It is with a feeling of enchantment and mystique when researching Hacienda de las Flores in Moraga that we learn the original 13,318.13 acres around it were named "Rancho Laguna de los Palos Colorados." Translated it means "Ranch of the Lake of the Redwoods." In the late 1700s it was a hunting ground of the Acalanes Indian tribe. The rancho was granted to the grandson of the founder of San Francisco (1776) and to his cousin, Juan Bernal, in 1835.

The grandson had been named after his illustrious ancestor, Jose Joaquin Moraga, but the rancho grantee's second name was embellished with the name of the ecclesiastical feast on which he was baptized: "de la Santisima Trinidad."

He constructed his adobe ranchhouse in 1841, and added to it as the number of children of his son, Jose de Jesus, increased. About a mile west of the Hacienda, it is a private residence today and is the oldest structure in Contra Costa County.

In the early 1850s squatters took over part of the rancho land. One of them was Jesse Hall Williams of Virginia, who squatted on this spot in 1854. However, in 1857 he was forced by the County to purchase these 160 acres from Jose de Jesus for $800. Williams' son Albert sold the quarter section in 1906 to the Manuel Lucas family.

Moraga brand

In 1916 the farmhouse and twenty acres were sold to two maiden ladies, Gertrude Mallette and Alberta H. Higgins, both from the east. They wanted to provide a home for orphaned children, which was never allowed. They hired two architects, Bakewell and Weihe of San Francisco, to design a Spanish ranch-style single story house of three bedrooms, with oak floors and Spanish tile roof.

These two young women ran this ranch, raising prize cattle, sheep and Irish setters and some crops. Miss Gertrude E. Mallette was the designer of the original Hacienda structure. She was a nurse at Stanford Hospital and authored more than twenty-five children's books. She also wrote for the *Oakland Tribune*. Miss Alberta H. Higgins was accepted socially in the Bay Area cities.

With the crash of 1929, they were forced to sell the property. On December 24, 1934, Donald Rheem, son of William S. Rheem, 1917-18 president* of Standard Oil of California, purchased the house and sixteen acres for a summer home. He transformed the country farmhouse into the "San Simeon of the East Bay." To the main structure he

Hacienda de las Flores in Moraga.

68

added the second floor of two wings and added a fourth wing to the rear. In all there were eighteen rooms in this Spanish styled "Hacienda*, designed by architect Clarence Tantau in the style of the 1930s.

The ironwork, ceramic tile, leather, mahogany and dark oak woods, silver and gold leaf, arched windows, staircases, crystal chandeliers and many mirrors were used in the remodeling. In addition Rheem constructed a swimming pool with a four-room cabana, bar and salon, race track and stable. There was also a chauffeur's residence, maid and butler's quarters, guest bedrooms, theatre with darkroom and kitchen. The estate was magnificently landscaped, with many trees from the 1939-40 Golden Gate International Exposition on San Francisco Bay.

A two-story "castle" chalet above the estate never materialized because of the scarcity of materials during World War II and imposed earthquake standards. Rheem had spent $30,000 on its design and construction, which was not completed. In 1970 the Richard Segners purchased the "castle" property and constructed a modern home on the foundation.

In 1961, after spending $600,000 on this week-end summer bungalow, Donald Rheem sold the estate to the Christian Brothers for $225,000. They used the home as their western headquarters. The new "De La Salle Institute" was converted into offices and multi-use areas. The former mansion solarium was converted into the chapel. By this time the thirty-six-acre estate was only nine and six-tenths acres.

Finding the place too ostentatious and receiving criticism from their confreres in this respect, the brothers put it up for sale. They were there for seventeen years, from 1961 to 1978. However, between 1972 and 1978 they used only the north wing and the office building. The latter was transformed by the Moraga Parks and Recreation Authority into a Senior Citizen Center. The estate was sold to the Moraga Parks and Recreation Authority for $343,750. They renamed it "Hacienda de las Flores," translated to "House of the Flowers." It was developed into recreational facilities. On November 1, 1977, the town council incorporated the authority and its properties as a town agency. The park included several buildings and botanical displays; the mansion was remodelled to serve as a cultural center. The former five-

car garage and living quarters served as the first town hall of Moraga, from November 13, 1974 to March 31, 1975. It is now a visual arts center.

The Hacienda de las Flores is open daily for public use. Private parties, weddings and receptions are also held there, under the auspices of the Moraga Park and Recreation Commission.

*Author's footnotes: My thanks to Priscilla Howard and Brother Dennis of Saint Mary's College, History Department, for use of some of this information, and my longtime friend Naomi Williams, who hostesses there on occasion. And further acknowledgements to Brother Dennis for corrections and updating.

The Standard Oil Company of California was founded about 1906. William S. Rheem died in 1919 and was not the company founder, as rumored.

Spanish styled "hacienda"—not as we know it in California hacienda structure.

OLD SAINT RAYMOND'S CHURCH
6506 DONLON WAY, DUBLIN

The old Saint Raymond's Church in Dublin is the oldest extant Catholic church building in Alameda County. It is now owned by the Amador-Livermore Historical Society. It was built in 1859 on land donated by Jeremiah Fallon and Michael Murray, who had been part of the ill-fated Donner Party, but left at Fort Bridger. They both came to the Dublin area in 1852. On April 22, 1860, the church dedication was under the invocation of Saint Raymond. It is located next to the Dublin Heritage Center at 6500 Donlon Way.

The old Dublin Cemetery is in the rear of the church and was formally established in 1859, although persons were buried in the area before that date. Many early pioneers and their descendants from the Amador, Livermore and San Ramon valleys are at rest there. The cemetery is still in use.

The Dublin Grammar School, built in 1856, was moved near the church and cemetery and became a part of this Dublin Heritage Center. E Clampus

Vitus, Joaquin Murrietta Chapter, dedicated the center at ceremonies held October 15, 1977.*

Old Saint Raymond's Church has been designated as Alameda County Point of Historical Interest Number 001. The Dublin Historical Preservation Association governs the Dublin Heritage Center.

Dublin—How it got its name: Dublin was first called Dougherty or Dougherty Station, after an inn of that same name built in 1862 on what is now the northside of Dublin Boulevard, and after Irish immigrant James Witt Dougherty. It was later changed to Dublin in respect for the homeland where many of its immigrants had their roots, as early as 1878.

*Author's footnotes: October 15, 1977, I was present at the dedication ceremonies and had a display of our San Ramon Valley Historical Society photographs there, as well as our historical post cards and my first book *Remembering Alamo...And Other Things Along the Way,* 1975.

My thanks to Ann Doss, curator, Amador-Livermore Valley Historical Society Museum.

Old Saint Raymond's Church in Dublin.

PLEASANTON HOTEL
855 MAIN STREET, PLEASANTON

The Farmer's Hotel was built by John W. Kottinger, known as the "father of Pleasanton," in 1864, on the creek bank. It opened for operation in 1865. A well and tank house were in the back, and a general store was located in the front. Kottinger, an Austrian, married Maria Refugia Bernal, the daughter of Juan Pablo Bernal, in 1850.

Kottinger sold to Herman Detjens, who came to Pleasanton in 1868 from San Francisco. He took charge of the Farmer's Hotel and ran it until the fall of 1874-75, when he began the erection of the Pleasanton Hotel, which was built prior to 1871. In 1887 there were three hotels in Pleasanton, according to the *San Francisco Journal of Commerce,* November 1887.

A Mr. Jordan and Jacob Johnson were also listed as owners, as well as the Bruss Brothers as hotelkeepers. Henry Reimers married the widow Bruss and then they owned the Farmer's Hotel. Reimers was first connected with the Pleasanton Hotel before he took over the Farmer's Hotel, which burned to the ground March 18, 1898. Reimers was a member of the town board of trustees and host at the Farmer's Hotel, an always popular and well-filled public house. He came to California from Germany in 1883 and became owner of the hotel in 1891.

In "Resources of Pleasanton," dated 1893-94, it is interesting to note prices at that time: board and lodging, five dollars and six dollars per week or one dollar per day; lodging, twenty-five cents and fifty cents; single meals, twenty-five cents.

Reimers immediately began to build on the original site. The hotel was on a sixty-four-foot frontage with a depth of forty-four feet. The upper floor had fourteen nicely furnished rooms and the lower floor was the dining room, bar, etc. Mr. and Mrs. Reimers had their apartment in the front room on the left, which later became the dining room for the establishment. They had four rooms—a living room, entrance hall, kitchen and bedroom. The hotel had electric lights.

In 1915 there was a second fire, which destroyed the rear area which at that time was the dining room. Sometime in the 1920s the hotel was called the Riverside Hotel. The Pleasanton Hotel burned in the early 1930s, and the Farmer's Hotel took that name sometime in the 1940s or 1950s. It was listed as the Farmer's Hotel with Henry Reimers as

Pleasanton Hotel in Pleasanton.

proprietor in 1932, according to the *Pleasanton Times*, 1930-34.

Owner of the hotel in 1960 was Robert Mason, and it was a fish restaurant with a nautical design to the dining room.

Terry Hufft owned it from 1969 to 1976. Mrs. Hufft did extensive work in the large garden areas, and a back portion was added in 1973. The owner in 1977 was Wanda J. Pollard. Owners in 1978 were Ava Ruth Willis and W. J. Pollard. In 1981 the owner listed was Better Restaurants, Inc.

George Martinovich of Alamo was the owner in 1981. He was also the owner of the Elegant Farmer in Oakland, and did considerable remodeling to the interior and added on to the back right side. The kitchen remodeling was about $250,000 for new insulation, non-skid floors and equipment. A twenty- by forty-foot extension of the bar for a dancing floor was built, and a brand new bar, as the old one fell apart during the dismantling and refinishing of the columned-mirrored back section. Everything was new from the ceiling to the carpets, with new booths, tables and offices. The interior designer was Margo Graham, who kept the hotel's heritage atmosphere. Martinovich gave the grand old hotel a new lease on life. In 1983 the business was purchased by Bill Laube.

Author's footnotes: How Pleasanton got its name— Pleasanton was called Alisal in its early history. Kottinger renamed it in honor of General Alfred Pleasonton, a Civil War officer of the Union Cavalry division of Major George Gordon Meade's Army of the Potomac. When Kottinger had the town surveyed and laid out, the two "o" spelling, it was said, was a county clerk error, so it became Pleasanton, as we know it today.

My thanks to Herb Hagemann for research and Ann Doss, curator of Amador-Livermore Valley Historical Society Museum, for some of this information and their permission for its use.

JOHN MARSH "STONE HOUSE"
MARSH CREEK ROAD, BRENTWOOD

John Marsh was born in Danvers, Massachusetts in 1799, descendant of an early New England family. He was a graduate of Harvard in 1823. He was thoroughly trained as a physician and surgeon, but had no formal medical degree, as the doctor under whom he apprenticed died. He was a man of culture and education. In cooperation with his French Canadian-Sioux Indian common-law wife, Marguerite Decouteaux of Wisconsin, they produced a dictionary and grammar of the Sioux language. He left Wisconsin following her death to begin life anew, leaving their son Charles with friends for care.

Dr. Marsh arrived in California in 1836 and was the first physician to start practice in Southern California. In 1837 he purchased a large Mexican land grant, Rancho Los Meganos, from Jose Noriega, near the San Joaquin River, for $500. Dr. Marsh's glowing letters about California written to his friends were widely published in newspapers in the midwest and east and influenced the organization of the Bidwell-Bartleson party of 1841, first to cross the Sierra into California. Dr. Marsh's rancho became the main stopping place between Sutter's Fort and the San Francisco Bay Area. His letter to Senator Lewis Cass, written February 1, 1846, came to the attention of President Polk.

On June 24, 1851 Dr. Marsh married Abigail (Abby) Smith Tuck of Massachusetts, a teacher of a girls' school in Santa Clara. They had a daughter Alice Frances, born March 1852, and he began the construction of the large stone baronial manor for them. He named it "Brentwood" after his ancestral lands in England. Before it could be finished his wife died of tuberculosis, in 1855. On September 24, 1856, when driving his horse and buggy from his ranch, he was assassinated by three ranch hands at Vine Hill, beyond Pacheco near Martinez. They were Juan Garcia, Felipe Morena and Jose Olivas. Marsh was fifty-seven years old. David McClure, missionary preacher/teacher, conducted the funeral services.

The architect for the stone house was Thomas Boyd, Esquire. He used the old English domestic style with a union of manor house and castle. There were arched windows, peaked roofs, projecting eaves, gables, a sixty-five-foot central tower to the three-story building. It was made of buff-colored Benicia stone quarried at the site, and corners, door and window jambs, sills and caps were laid with rubble-stone. Dimensions were sixty by forty feet, with three gable windows looking east, west and south. Sixteen rooms were enclosed by a ten-foot piazza which encircled three sides and was supported by octagon pillars. A living room, dining room and large hall were on the first floor. The large bedroom suite was on the second floor, and the third floor was all large bedrooms. The contractors were Pierce and Wood, and the entire cost was $20,000.

Following the estate settlement, the only members of the Marsh family to live in the house were son Charles and his wife Sarah (Pantier) and their five children, the two youngest born there. When Sarah died in 1865, her widower and the children moved to Antioch. Then he and his half-sister Alice sold the property and it was in litigation for years.

In 1878 Marco B. Ivory of Green Valley, Danville, a retired sheriff, was appointed superintendent and with his family lived there over twenty years. There were 13,000 acres in pasture, which he partially planted in wheat with good returns.

In May 1960, the Stone House was donated by the S. H. Cowell estate to Contra Costa County. In 1974 the house was added to the National Register of Historic Places. Restoration has had many delays and problems, because of its strange structure. Vandals have added to its ramshackled appearance. Estimates to properly restore it have been $685,000 and upward.

Governor Brown signed a bill authored by Assemblyman Dan Boatwright on September 28, 1978, allocating $1.5 million of state Collier Park Preservation Fund money to develop and restore the John Marsh Stone House. There were three requirements to be met, now paritally completed. Contra Costa County has given the deed to the house and surrounding five and one-half acres to the state, but it has not been accepted yet, because of the necessary conditions to be met. The Department of Parks and Recreation has a written agreement with Flood Control for public use of the reservoir, but it has not been finalized with the S. H. Cowell Foundation. Caretakers have a difficult time with trespassing and vandalism, which Pearl Silva, who lived there five years, says happens daily. John Casey, president pro-tem of the John Marsh Memorial Association, said vandalism

John Marsh's "Stone House" was completed in 1856. This photograph was taken before the earthquake of 1868.

and trespassing are "a sign of the times." If the area becomes a state historical park, supervision by state officials such as rangers and firemen would help to preserve this historical landmark architectural masterpiece.

Author's footnotes: My thanks to the late Father William N. Abeloe for some of this material, and also to Diane Alexander, branch librarian at Brentwood Library. And, Barbara Bonnickson of Brentwood advised that the John Marsh Memorial Association, Inc. is awaiting appointment of a new director of state parks. The president moved out of state, Barbara Bonnickson is vice-president, Joanne Dean is secretary, and Bob Gromm is treasurer. A meeting was held in mid-July 1983.

JOEL CLAYTON HOUSE
6101 MAIN STREET, CLAYTON

Joel Clayton was the eldest of twelve children. His family lived in a stone house on Briarly Green Farm, Darbyshire, England. His father was a lead miner and farmer. Joel became a mining engineer. He traveled throughout the British Isles to learn his trade, and arrived in America at the age of

twenty-seven in 1837. When he left Lowell, Massachusetts, he lived with an uncle in Pittsburg, Pennsylvania, and later with his brother William, who had a farm near Saint Louis, Missouri. Clayton, Missouri was founded by this Clayton family.

Joel Clayton's granddaughter, Edna Laurel Calhan, says in 1842 Joel was with trappers and prospectors when he first saw the beautiful valley at the base of Mount Diablo and said, "Some day this shall be my home."

His wife and their three small children joined him in California, where for three years they ran a stage station in the Tehachapi Mountains. In 1853, after a dairy farm in San Francisco, Joel obtained forty acres from E. B. Clark, in what is now Mitchell Canyon. He added to this via the Homestead Act of 1862 and other purchases. In 1857, at the age of forty-seven, he plotted and laid out the Clayton townsite.

He was the areas's first subdivider, building, selling lots and promoting town commerce. He built his second home in the valley of Mount Diablo and Mitchell creeks, and planted hay, grain and grapes and operated a dairy ranch. Joel

73

Clayton died of pneumonia in 1872 at Somersville and is buried in the family plot at Live Oak Cemetery.

The true date the house was built is not on record. However, it appeared on County records in 1880. Longtimers say it has been known as "Liberty House" and "Keller House."

A man named Liberty lived there with his young daughter Elodia, after he and his wife separated. Elodia married Charles Henry Keller in 1897. They lived in Concord, where he operated a butcher shop. In the early 1900s Henry Keller, Sr. moved in.

The house was moved to the north side of the creek in 1916, at the rear of a larger new home the younger Kellers built in 1912. It was separated and moved with the use of one horse and wooden rollers. It has been used as a guest house, bunkhouse and office building, with additions, alterations and updating. Construction changes are noted on the east side of the building. At one time

Joel Clayton house in Clayton, now the Clayton Historical Society Museum. The drawing is by Jewell Leavitt.

it had a veranda (piazza) across the front, later replaced with a small covered porch.

In 1975 the house was moved to its third and present site at 6101 Main Street, next door to the Pioneer Inn. The Pacific Coast Development Company gave the house to the Clayton Historical Society, which is attempting to furnish it as a typical modest Victorian era ranch home.

An annual Camellia Tea is held on the Sunday closest to Valentine's Day, to honor all descendants of pioneer families. The museum is open on Wednesdays and Sundays from 2:00 to 4:00 P.M.

Author's footnotes: My thanks for materials written by Eldora Hoyer of Clayton, sent for my use by museum curator Constance M. Rehr.

The town was named for Joel Clayton. Its post office dates from 1857. The town was incorporated in 1964.

An early visitor to Clayton was Jedediah Strong Smith, explorer, trapper and preacher. He was the man who opened up the central overland trail. He came to the Clayton area in 1826.

GALINDO HOME
1721 AMADOR AVENUE, CONCORD

Don Salvio Pacheco was a native Californian whose grandfather came to California with Captain Juan Bautista de Anza's expedition in 1776. Salvio Pacheco was alcalde and held other posts while in San Jose. He petitioned for a land grant, calling the area Monte del Diablo (meaning a willow thicket) which was near the northern edge of Concord. It was rumored to be an Indian burial ground.

In 1834, he was granted the land, an area of 17,921 acres. He put his eldest son Fernando in charge. About 1849 Don Salvio and his wife Juana and the family moved there to live. The property had beautiful streams and many oak trees. He built an adobe there, and it became the center for activities and hospitality. There was also a brick-lined swimming pool and bull ring.

These pioneers raised cattle and sheep, followed by grain and fruit trees, and they also bred horses. The town of Pacheco was named for Don Salvio Pacheco. In its early history it was a shipping point, but the earthquake in 1868 ceased that activity there.

Don Salvio Pacheco started a new town on his property, calling it "Todos Santos" (All Saints). It later was changed to Concord, which means "harmony," and Concord it has remained.

The Galindo home was built in the 1850s. The great-great granddaughter of Don Salvio Pacheco, Miss Ruth Galindo, whose family has a street named for them, has lived there all her life. She, her brother Harold and sister Leonora Fink were born there.

She is president of the Concord Historical Society and served many years as a director of the Contra Costa County Historical Society. She retired from teaching in 1972—it was only natural that she taught Spanish.

The Galindo home was built in the 1850s. This photograph was taken in the 1880s.

Galindo home. (Courtesy Oakland Tribune)

JOHN MUIR HOME
4202 ALHAMBRA AVENUE, MARTINEZ

John Muir was born April 21, 1838, in Dunbar Scotland, one of eight children. His Calvinist father, who used daily stern paternal discipline, was a shopkeeper. In 1849, with his father, brother David and sister Sarah, John arrived in southern Wisconsin, a few miles from Portage on a sunny hill above Fountain Lake. His father built them a log hut. The mother and four other children arrived later. John toiled there for ten years, preparing for the day he would be free to explore the great world. One autumn day in 1860 he bid goodbye and turned up at the state fair in Madison. He entered the University of Wisconsin, studying literature, botany, chemistry and geology. His room in Old North Hall became a show place of plants in pots and presses, rocks, birds' nests, insect chrysalises and more. After four years of learning he left for the "University of the Wilderness," via the Great Lakes up into Canada. He went to work in a broom and rake factory in County Grey. When the factory burned he earned his living in an Indianapolis machine shop until a steel file almost blinded him. So he set out for the Gulf of Mexico, via Georgia and Florida, and became ill with malaria. He then went to Cuba and sailed for New York, where he booked passage for California.

In March 1868 he landed in San Francisco and "drifted" to the Sierra, which he viewed from Pacheco Pass, while at his feet lay the San Joaquin Valley. For ten years he headquartered in the Yosemite Valley, living on tea, raw oatmeal, berries and nuts. By night he began to write. Through his longtime friend, Jeanne Carr (Mrs. Ezra S.), his writings appeared in the *New York Tribune*, *Harper's Monthly*, and *The Overland*. Within three years this unknown was being sought after. In 1871 came Emerson, followed by Agassiz, Asa Gray, Joseph Le Conte, Sir Joseph Hooker and others.

For thirteen years Muir alone championed the trees. On a summer night in 1889 he camped near Soda Springs in the Tuolumne Meadows with Robert Underwood Johnson, editor of the *Century* magazine. they talked of saving Yosemite by having the government take it over. Muir outlined the park boundaries and wrote the articles, and Johnson drafted a bill to establish Yosemite National Park. On October 1, 1890, the bill passed both houses. Out of the same urge, the General Grant and Sequoia national parks were created and forest reserves of 13 million acres set aside. John Muir's first book, *Mountains of California*, was published. President Theodore Roosevelt, in the spring of 1903, tramped Yosemite with Muir, for three days and nights. He returned to Washington to inaugurate an aggressive conservation policy. During his term of office, 148 million acres of forest domains were added, creating five national parks and sixteen national monuments.

Muir's silent partner in his work was his wife Louie (Strentzel), daughter of Dr. John Strentzel and his wife Louisiana. Strentzel, a medical doctor, was a Polish revolutionary, a Texas frontiersman and a forty-niner before he settled to the life of a fruit rancher in Alhambra Valley, a pioneer horticulturist and California landowner. In April 1880 Muir and Louie were married, and part of the

The John Muir home in Martinez is now a national historic site.

77

Strentzel ranch in Contra Costa County was her father's wedding gift to them. They had two daughters, Wanda and Helen, who were educated at home by live-in governesses.

Louie Muir was a rare, understanding woman, a gracious homemaker and an accomplished pianist. She was a lover of flowers and had a keen interest in scientific invention. As time went by, she became Muir's most trusted literary adviser. He published nothing without her approval. She helped him live his two lives harmoniously.

John Muir spent part of every year traveling. As a youth he would sign his notebooks with "John Muir, Earth-Planet, Universe." In his seventy-six years he joyfully explored "this blessed star."

The John Muir Home was built in 1882 for John and Louisiana Strentzel. When Dr. Strentzel died in 1890, the Muirs moved into the big house. The three-story house has seven fireplaces for heat, twelve-foot ceilings, a basement, attic and bell-tower, and close to twenty rooms. The house cost $9,500; however, extras like plumbing and the fireplaces brought the final cost closer to $20,000. Muir installed electricity to replace the kerosene lamps just before he died in 1914. When he was not in the mountains, much of his writing was done from the study on the second floor. Muir died December 24, 1914 in Los Angeles. His wife had died in 1905.

Through the efforts of the John Muir Memorial Association, the home was declared a national historic site in 1964. The National Park Service is restoring the building and grounds to reflect the period between 1906 and 1914 as nearly as possible. The house is open daily except on Thanksgiving, Christmas and New Year's days, for self-guided tours. Groups can arrange for tours in advance. A film about John Muir's life and philosophy is shown hourly.

CAMEL BARNS
INDUSTRIAL PARK AND PORT FACILITY
BENICIA

On May 19, 1847, Dr. Robert Semple, Thomas O. Larkin and General Mariano Guadaloupe Vallejo agreed to form the town of Benicia. It was named for the general's wife, Dona Maria Francesca Benicia Felipe Carrillo de Vallejo. On April 30, 1849, the United States Army established the Benicia Barracks. Their 115-year tenure ended on March 31, 1964, when the Benicia Arsenal was deactivated.*

Several of the arsenal's original buildings still stand and are being preserved, restored and renovated, for historical significance. They are available for viewing to schools, historical societies and other interested groups. Among them are: the guard house, 1872; clock tower, 1859; commandant's home, 1860; powder magazine, 1857; post hospital, 1856; post cemetery, 1849; and the camel barns, 1853-54.

The camel barns were constructed with walls two and one-half feet thick, made of hand-hewn sandstone quarried from the military site. Some brick and wood were also used, and the roof was of corrugated sheet metal. This massive, austere styling was used for most of the buildings, whose designer is unknown.

In the 1860s these early warehouse buildings were given the name "Camel Barns." The United States Camel Corps purchased a herd of camels in 1855 for military use in the American southwest desert states. Jefferson Davis, Secretary of War under President Franklin Pierce, persuaded Congress to purchase over thirty camels from the eastern Mediterranean for $30,000. They were brought via ship on the three-month trip to Indianola, Texas. Strangely, only one died and two new colts were born en route. Later they were stabled at Fort Tejon in Southern California. After years of experimenting, in September 1863 Quartermaster General E. B. Babbitt ordered that the thirty-five camels be sold. They were driven from Southern California, reaching Benicia in February 1864. Can you imagine this caravan on the long trek? Of course people stared, horses reared, dogs barked, cattle stampeded, and the camels spat! They crossed the Berkeley hills to Martinez, where, a few at a time, they boarded the ferry boat.

On February 28, 1864, they were sold at auction at the Benicia arsenal. All of them were purchased by Samuel McLeneghan, one of the camel drivers. He hoped to race them against horses to make some quick money. An Arab, Hadj Ali, called "Hi Jolly" by the American soldiers, was hired to get the camels over the Sierra Nevada mountains. During some transactions McLeneghan disappeared and "Hi Jolly" took ownership of the herd. He sold them to zoos and circuses. It is said the last camel died in Los Angeles Griffith Park in 1934.

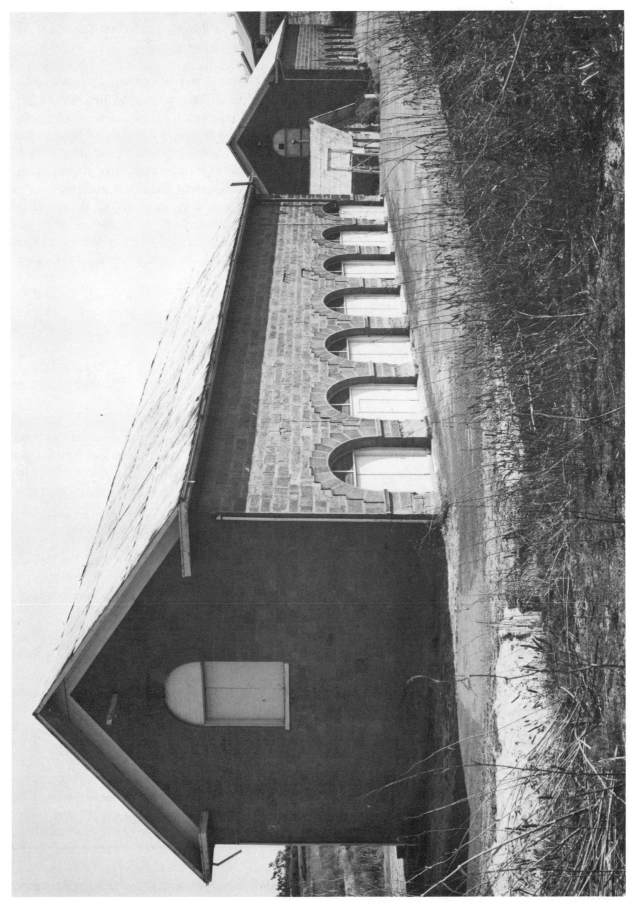

The camel barns at the arsenal in Benicia. (Photograph by James E. Simonsen, Applied Arts, Benicia, © 1983)

The camel barns are owned by the city of Benicia and listed on the National Register of Historic Places. They were recently given to the Benicia Historical and Cultural Museum Foundation. The trustees are in the process of cleaning and repairing the building to use for a city museum.

*Author's footnotes: Benicia arsenal deactivated March 31, 1964—At the time the last commandant was Colonel Lewis Andrews Nickerson, who served two tours of duty there, from 1933 to 1937 and again in the 1960s. His son Richard "Nick" Nickerson of South Avenue, Alamo, met his wife Elinor "Lin" Barkley, a Benicia native, while in high school there. They have been neighbors of mine for years. Their oldest son Steve and my son Gary were in the same grade in school. While Colonel Nickerson was there he helped to refurbish the buildings. It was interesting to learn there is a tunnel connecting some of these buildings and a basement where slaves were held.

My thanks to Peggy Dunbar Martin and trustee Frances Preissner, who sent material for my use, and Benicia Industries, Inc., for my conversations with personnel there.

FERNANDEZ MANSION
100 TENNENT AVENUE, PINOLE

Bernardo Fernandez was born in Portugal in 1827. He sailed the seas, including ports of Africa and South America, on freighters from the age of thirteen. In 1853 he came around the Horn and arrived in the port of San Francisco. In 1854 he settled on the waterfront of Pinole.* He bought property from Dr. Samuel Tennent, for whom the street was named. There he started a mercantile business and supply store. Fernandez prospered and owned grain warehouses, vessels and real estate which eventually totaled some twenty thousand acres in Pinole.

In 1859 he married Carlotta Cuadra of Marin County, whose family was originally from Valparaiso, Chili. Her father was an early pioneer to the Marin County area. They were married in Saint Mary's Catholic Church in San Francisco in December 1859. They had six children, three boys and three girls. They were: Maria Antonia "Mamie," who never married; Anita, who married Captain C. W. Sinclair and had no children; Bernardo, who died when he was twenty and never married; Emelia, who married William K. Cole and had five children; Manuel, who married Bernice Burch and had three children; Thomas, who married

Ottile Riepling and had two children. Several of the descendants have made their homes in the Pinole area over the years.

The house of this piece was the third one built on the property. The first house was destroyed by floods in 1862 and the second by fire in the 1890s. Fernandez built their third home overlooking San Pablo Bay. It was a two-story wood frame mansion with over twenty rooms and a tower. Its design is considered a fine example of sixteenth century Classic Mannerist Italianate architecture* of northern Italy. They celebrated their fiftieth wedding anniversary in the home in 1909, and many who had attended their wedding were in attendance. Bernardo died in 1912, at the age of eighty-five.

Members of the Fernandez family owned the mansion until the 1930s. It then had a series of owners. During the 1950s it was taken over by some "beatniks."

Since 1970 it has belonged to Dr. Joseph Mariotti and his wife Gretchen, who repaired and restored the rundown home. They gift-deeded it to the city of Pinole in December 1973. The house on two and one-half acres is listed in the National Register of Historic Places and is California Point of Historical Interest #C Co-6. It was so dedicated with a plaque November 14, 1976, the bicentennial year, which reads:

Fernandez Mansion 1894-1976

This monument marks the site of Pinole's birthplace and the center of its activities until the early 20th century. The beginning of Pinole was built on the waterfront and around the mouth of Pinole Creek during the latter half of the 19th century. During the 1850s Bernardo Fernandez started a mercantile business on this site. Here he built a supply store, constructed warehouses and wharves, hauled farm products and handled the mail to become very instrumental in the early establishment of this city. The Fernandez Mansion, a California Point of Historical Interest, marks the remnant of Pinole's birthplace and shall be preserved in perpetuity!

Dedicated 1976.

*Author's footnote: Pinole, from the Mexican grant El Rancho Pinole. Though some say the Indians fed

The Fernandez mansion in Pinole, built in 1894. (Photo courtesy Dr. Joseph Mariotti)

some explorers a meal mix they called "pinola."

Architecture—From a paper prepared by A. Lewis Kone, FAIA, the two-story wood frame over brick full basement with attic rooms—Main floor reached by eight foot wide monumental exterior stairway with banister of turned balisters and moulded handrail. Covered porch and exterior vestibule which projects from building and extends up throughout second story terminating with a truncated pyramidal mansarded roof. Main block of house is approximately forty-one feet square sheathed with rustic siding and crowned with a classic cornice supported by handsawn brackets composed with window architraves. Main entrance motif flanked by coupled windows and three-story bay windows superimposed with triangular pediments composed with the main cornice. Ceiling height of main floor is twelve feet, second floor eleven feet and basement eight feet. Interior has panelled wood wainscot, plate rails, beam ceilings, wallpapers, fireplaces and many other features too innumerable to include.

ALVARADO ADOBE
NUMBER ONE ALVARADO SQUARE
SAN PABLO

Juan Bautista Alvarado was born in Monterey, the capital of Alta California, in 1809. He was a protege of Governor Sola and an eager student. At eighteen he became secretary to the Diputacion. He was administrator of customs in 1845 after being an appraiser from 1834. At twenty-six he became a member of the Diputacion, and its president at twenty-seven. With the overthrow of Gutierrez, Alvarado was the first native-born governor of California. Mexico appointed him constitutional governor in 1840. When California became a state he retired from public life, though not totally averse to the American takeover. He married Martina Castro in 1839 and with their six children settled in San Pablo.

The Alvarado Adobe was built by Jesus Maria Castro for his mother, Dona Gabriela Berryesse de Castro, widow of Francisco Castro, the grantee of Rancho San Pablo. It was first occupied in the early 1840s. It became the home of Gabriela's youngest daughter, Martina, and her husband Alvarado. He altered the adobe with the addition of clapboards, redwood shingles and a fireplace, and surrounded the home with orchards, hay fields, grape arbors, roses and shrubbery. Alvarado died in 1882. He had lived in the adobe thirty-seven years. Later the adobe was sold and used by a general store for storage. In 1954 it was razed and replaced with an apartment house.

The Alvarado Adobe is a replica* and has been completely reconstructed, with 10,000 adobe bricks. It opened in November 1978* and is administered by the San Pablo Historical and Museum Society. Alvarado Square also houses the offices of the City of San Pablo. It was constructed with funds from the Public Works and Employment Act of 1976, the San Pablo Redevelopment Agency and the City of San Pablo.

The Alvarado Adobe is open to the public at no charge on Saturday and Sunday afternoons from one o'clock to five o'clock. School groups and tours can be arranged during the week.

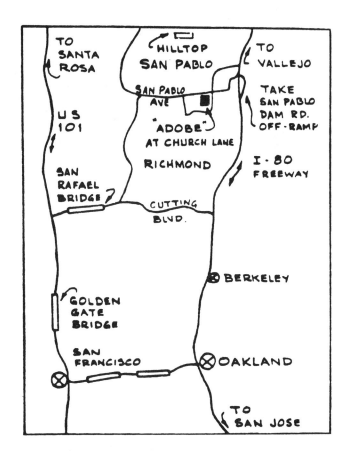

Alvarado Adobe
San Pablo

A 1981 photo of Alvarado Adobe by Roger Rehm.

BLUME HOUSE MUSEUM

Henry Blume was born in Westphalia, Prussia in 1837. In 1856 he came to San Francisco and purchased land in San Pablo a few years later. In 1867 he married Frederika Johanning, also of Germany. They had five sons, Henry, Frederick, William, Charles and Albert. The family purchased over one thousand acres in the northern section of Rancho San Pablo from the Emeric holdings. Here they farmed for over fifty years. In 1911 Blume sold to Standard Oil for their tank farm operations, reserving thirty-six acres, and leased back 400 acres for farming with main crops in hay and grain. They also had cattle, milk cows and chickens, and sold to local markets and the community. They also kept pigs, rabbits, guinea hens, peacocks, pigeons and bees. Their sons were educated at Hill School.

The Blume House was built in 1905 and was complete with running water, served by a 6,000 gallon tank and windmill. There were seven bedrooms, a parlor, kitchen, dining room and two bathrooms. A fireplace and kitchen stove supplied the heat. In 1929 the acetylene gas lighting system was replaced with electricity. Out buildings were two barns, a bunkhouse, chicken house, egg house, dairy house, granary, blacksmith shop and tool shed.

Henry Blume died in 1895, but his widow and her sons ran the farm until the late 1940s. Later a series of renters raised sheep and horses on the land. Chevron Land and Development Corporation picked up the option on the remaining homestead acres, and in 1970 plans began for the Hilltop Mall Shopping Center. The San Pablo Historical Society came into existence at that time for the

The Blume House.

purpose of preserving the old farmhouse and turning it into a museum. Chevron donated the house and the bunkhouse to the City of San Pablo, paying the expenses of moving the two buildings to Alvarado Square in 1974. Through shared community effort, the house was furnished and refurbished over the years, and opened to the public in 1979.

*Author's footnotes: Replica—I used two buildings in this piece, because they both go together and tell San Pablo's early history, and because of all the combined effort of the many participants to restore, preserve and reconstruct the adobe.

November 1978—Some members of the San Ramon Valley Historical Society, including myself, attended a dinner meeting and tour of the Alvarado Adobe and Square soon after it opened.

My thanks to Ann Roberts, who sent photos and much information for my use.

It is interesting to note that the three museums open to the public which I've included in this chapter progressed because of the sons-in-law, i.e. Alvarado, John Muir and Albert M. Johnson (of Shadelands). This coincidence was pointed out to me by Bev Clemson of Shadelands.

BANK OF RICHMOND
201 WEST RICHMOND AVENUE
RICHMOND

The Bank of Richmond was organized in 1902, and construction was begun on a large, prestigious building of yellow glazed brick at the corner of Washington and West Richmond avenues.

A staircase led from the sidewalk to the first floor. Offices were upstairs and there were shops along West Richmond Avenue. In 1910 the building was remodelled. An addition was built behind the bank on Washington Avenue. It was used for storage of books and papers. The floor of the bank was lowered to street level, eliminating the stairs. The pointed roof on the round bay in front was removed in the mid-1920s.

The Bank of Richmond continued until the early 1920s, when it became the First Richmond Branch Mercantile Trust Company. From the late 1920s to the mid 1930s it was the American Trust Company. In the early 1940s it was a billiard hall called "Bank Club Billiards," for a time.

Over the years many different businesses occupied the storefronts in the bank building along West Richmond Avenue. Among them were the People's Water Company, McWhorter's Grocery, Brother's "Groceteria," W. B. Jenkins, a tailor,

Wood and Wood Notions, a beauty shop and a barber shop.

There were offices above the bank and in 1902 it was the early telephone exchange. Dr. Abbott, the coroner, was located there around 1912, and in 1914 he opened the Emergency Hospital over the bank when he closed the hospital on West Richmond. In the early 1920s the offices were converted to lodgings, at one time called the Bank Hotel and later the Hartynyk Hotel.

In the mid 1950s Bob and Sherry Hartynyk bought the building, and the upper floor became their home. They moved their variety store to the street level. Mrs. Hartynyk began a boutique in the rear of the store, while she raised their two children. Mr. Hartynyk passed away in 1979, and his widow and son and daughter continue the business.

Richmond City Hall and the Bank of Richmond, circa 1909. The bank was lowered to street level in 1910. Richmond's first newspaper, The Record, *was published in the bank basement until it was inundated with mud when a sewer clogged. (Courtesy Point Richmond History Association, Don Church Collection)*

RICHMOND CITY HALL
210 WASHINGTON, RICHMOND

By 1909 the city government of Richmond had outgrown the Critchett Hotel, so John Nicholl built 210 Washington, with its bell tower and flag pole on the roof. He used the upstairs for his offices and leased the ground floor for the city hall, for fifty dollars per month. The John Nicholl City Hall was used from 1909 to 1915, when the city offices required larger quarters and the lease had run out. On January 9, 1922, the Point Masonic Lodge bought the building for their lodge on the upper floor with a clubroom below. The Masonic

Order still meets there. Lola's Beauty Shop was downstairs for thirty years. The space is still used for a beauty shop.

Author's footnote: My thanks to Donna Roselius of Richmond, who sent material with photo for my use.

DUNSMUIR HOUSE
2960 PERALTA OAKS COURT, OAKLAND

Dunsmuir House was designed by J. Eugene Freeman, architect son of one of the Dunsmuir sea captains. It is in the Classic Revival Victorian style with massive Corinthian columns, a Greek pediment and Italian-style ornamentation. The house was completed in nine months in 1899, at a cost of $350,000. It has thirty-seven rooms with many tiled bathrooms, some with heated showers. There is no central heat, but ten fireplaces.

Dunsmuir House was built by Alexander White Dunsmuir, heir to a British Columbia coal mining and shipping fortune, for his intended bride, Mrs. Josephine Wallace. Because of her divorce, he dared not marry her and be disinherited by his mother. Because of this awkward circumstance,

they lived together for twenty years. He helped raise and educate her daughter, Edna Wallace Hopper, who was a New York stage star.

Alexander and his brother James bought out their mother's business interest and Alexander then purchased the 310-acre Souther Farm estate. He and Josephine finally married in 1899, in the town of San Pablo. Forty days after the marriage, on January 31, 1900, Alexander died. He was forty-six years old. Josephine followed eighteen months later, apparently of cancer. They are buried at Mountain View Cemetery in Oakland.

Her daughter Edna Wallace Hopper inherited

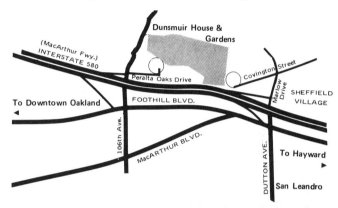

Dunsmuir House and Gardens in Oakland.

the estate and operated a vegetable and fruit farm for a few years. In 1906, unable to properly maintain the extensive property, she sold it to I. W. Hellman, Jr., son of the founder of Wells Fargo Bank, who was a San Francisco financier. He and his family enjoyed the estate as a summer home for the next fifty-five years, having sought refuge there following the 1906 San Francisco earthquake and fire.

In 1962, the City of Oakland purchased the Hellman Estate with funds from the sale of freeway rights to the State of California. Much of the original acreage was rezoned and sold, and about forty-eight acres remain. The City of Oakland had planned to develop a conference center on the site, but it was not feasible. In 1972, a non-profit corporation of volunteers was set up to help preserve and restore the property to a cultural, horticultural and historic center for the benefit of the public, and it became Dunsmuir House and Gardens, Inc.

The house has been reroofed and repainted, rooms repaired, parquet floors refinished and the stained Tiffany-type glass dome in the entry hall restored. The original wood and coal burning stove and the servants' call-box are still in the kitchen. Several proposed projects will continue to restore and preserve its superb architecture and share this old mansion with the public.

Dunsmuir House and Gardens is open on Sundays, Easter through September 12, noon to 4:00 P.M. and for special events and when rented out. There are several types of memberships, and fees and gifts are tax deductible.

Author's footnote: Over the years I've visited this lovely well-preserved home for benefit functions. In 1978 I enjoyed the "Carousel Christmas," which was the eighth annual Christmas Festival and featured hand-carved carousel animals in various rooms and a designer showcase. I was also the winner of a delightful Christmas gourmet basket.

McCONAGHY ESTATE
18701 HESPERIAN BOULEVARD
HAYWARD

Neal McConaghy came to America from Scotland in 1848. In 1858, with only five dollars, he arrived in San Lorenzo, California, to work on a ranch, where he saved his money and built a grist mill. In 1865, he acquired 197 acres and raised grain and vegetables. These he sent to the San Francisco market via steamer from Robert's Landing, at the foot of Lewelling Boulevard. Neal married Sarah McCaw in 1863. They built a home at the end of Grant Avenue, where they lived for twenty years. Their five children were born during that time.

In 1886, they built a house on Hesperian Boulevard in Hayward. The contractor was John Haar, Sr., later to become Hayward's mayor. It was a twelve-room farmhouse, with outbuildings of a tank house and carriage house. The carriage house has the original horse stalls, rooms for the farm stallion and for washing carriages. Above there is a huge hayloft. The house has an entry hall with a stairway to the second floor. Rooms are spacious with high ceilings and pastel-colored moldings. The main floor has the family parlor, dining room, butler's pantry, company parlor, library, kitchen and pantry. Four bedrooms are upstairs; one has a fireplace. The two back rooms were for the servants' use, with a staircase down to the kitchen. There is a large attic and a small basement under the kitchen area. During the 1906 San Francisco earthquake the chimney crumbled and fell through the skylight in the hall, leaving dents in the upstairs railing, still visible today. The roofline was then changed so the skylight is blocked from the outside.

John McConaghy, the youngest child, was fifteen years old when this house was built. He married Florence Smyth in about 1912 and planned to build their home on Bockman Road. But because his parents were ill, he brought his bride to the family home, in the manner of the extended family. John and Florence did not have any children. In 1972, John passed away at the age of 100. He left the house and ranch to the Crippled Children's Shrine Hospital.

In July 1973, efforts of citizens of Hayward and San Lorenzo, with the Hayward Area Recreation and Park District, started proceedings to purchase the property. The Hayward Area Historical Society agreed to assume responsibility for the house and developed it into a museum. The Hayward Area Recreation and Park District landscaped the grounds, in keeping with the adjacent Kennedy Park. The house has been restored room by room. Most recently it was painted with shades of blue grey to accent its architectural detail.

The estate is open Thursday, Friday, Saturday and Sunday from 1:00 to 4:00 P.M. Groups may

The McConaghy Estate, which was built in 1886.

tour by appointment. The house is decorated for "Christmas 1886" during the month of December. There are also special Victorian decorations for other holidays.

Author's footnote: My thanks to Lois Over, promotion director, for material sent for my use, and to Beulah E. Linnell for information.

GRIFFITH HOUSE
1063 CURTIS STREET, ALBANY

The city we now know as Albany, between Berkeley and El Cerrito, in its beginning was appropriately called Ocean View. It celebrated its seventy-fifth year September 22 to 25, 1983.*

David Thomas Griffith, a city electrical inspector for San Francisco, came to do the wiring for the Peralta Park Hotel in Ocean View. It was built for the actor Maurice Curtis, for whom the street was named, and completed in 1891. Griffith liked Ocean View so much but did not want to commute, so quit his inspector's job and started his own business as electrical contractor on Shattuck Avenue. He went to work on the steam train to Vine and Shattuck and walked the remaining way. There was also a horse car which went as far as Saint Joseph's School.

One of the earliest homes built in Albany was for David Thomas Griffith. This four-room house was built in 1893. It is in the southeast corner of Albany near the Berkeley line. The Griffiths had two children, a son Thomas and daughter Linnea. She might have been one of the earliest born in Ocean View, had there been medical facilities then. Her parents went to San Francisco for her October 20, 1898* arrival. At the age of five weeks she was returned to Curtis Street, which was across the street from her future husband Robert Andrew Hansen's 1062 Curtis Street home. That home was built by "Grandpa Hansen" in 1904, and is also still standing.

Curtis Street was then called Christiana, named for the tract. There was much open space available, with cows grazing, but the lots were laid out in twenty-five-foot parcels. The Griffiths owned six lots and one that went through to the street above called Neilsen.

Linnea first attended the two-room schoolhouse on Page Street near Seventh Street, past San Pablo Avenue. Later she went to Presentation School on Addison Street. She did not have any immediate

The McConaghy Mansion, Hayward, 1886

playmates her own age, on her side of the creek, which is the dividing line for Berkeley. There were, however, six Hagemen children and two Steinmetz boys living next door.

Linnea Griffith married Robert Hansen, who was born on Julia Street, Berkeley, April 30, 1893, on March 12, 1918. While living on Curtis Street they raised four children, Lorraine*, Robert, Jr., Thomas and Dorothy.

There have been several residents in this house over the years. The Pizzini family lived there for many years and their children attended local schools. This Griffith house was on the Albany Historical Society House Tour May 4, 1980.

The Robert Hansens still live in Albany, on Evelyn Street. He was ninety in April 1983 and she eighty-five in October. The Hansen offspring haven't ventured too far from their Albany roots. Thomas lives at 1068 Neilsen and Dorothy is on Spokane Avenue, with their families.

*Author's footnotes: Albany—My family and I moved to a rental on Adams Street, Albany, in 1925 from Oakland, and I attended second grade at Cornell School with Miss Brewer as my teacher. Early in 1926 we moved into our new home at 1085 Curtis Street in Albany, and I attended third grade at Marin School with Miss Foley as my teacher. I graduated from Marin Grammar School and went on to Herbert Hoover Junior High School in Albany and graduated at ninth grade level and then went to Berkeley High School. Herbert Hoover Junior High School later became Albany High School, as it is today. I resided with my family at the Curtis Street address, until I was married June 16, 1940, and with my husband moved to Virginia Street in Berkeley. I hold some interesting property deeds on a home I still own at 1069 Curtis Street. These cover Christiana Tract. The first one, dated August 5, 1895, is between Raymond A. Perry and his wife Winifred of Oakland, Alameda County, to J. A. Miller of San Francisco, for ten dollars in gold coin, on Lot #31, in Book "F" as laid down and delineated upon a certain map entitled "Amended Map of Christiana Tract," Berkeley, Alameda County, California. Subdivided by Geo. L. Nusbaumer C.E. County Surveyor, 1891. Filed for record May 19, 1891, in office of County Recorder of said Alameda County, recorded August 13, 1895, 564 of deeds page 233. March 10, 1910, J. A. Miller of San Francisco, for ten dollars in gold coin to Elise Emma Miller, including appurtenances. April 7, 1921, Mary E. Hudson and Frank B. Hudson, who sold to my stepfather John K. Chaplik October 1952 for my mother's birthday present. Recorded February 26, 1954 to them and on May 28, 1974 my mother Bertha M. Chaplik Boggini gifted to me, Virginia V. Jones. I still own this property. There have been several renters over the years, including: Albert R. Entelman, Jr., in

1952; Mr. and Mrs. C. Snyder in 1955; Mr. and Mrs. John E. Liggett in 1957; Mr. and Mrs. George Sorensen, 1958; and since February 24, 1959, Paul and Marian "Bly" Talkington, who remain as current residents. These early deeds will be donated to the Albany Historical Society.

September 22 to 25, 1983—I attended the tea honoring women in Albany's history, Friday, September 23, 1983 at the Baptist Church in Albany.

October 20, 1898—My mother Bertha Louis Boggini shared the same birthday and they were neighbors for over forty-five years.

Lorraine—She was my closest and dearest friend from 1926 and all through our school years and after. She was my maid of honor at my 1940 wedding, when I left Curtis Street. She passed away suddenly of cancer May 24, 1983, and is greatly missed by all. The Hansen family was my second family, as I grew up.

My thanks to Catherine J. Webb of Albany, who sent material and photo for my use.

The Griffith house at 1063 Curtis Street in Albany. (Courtesy Albany Historical Society, Ed McManus)

Epilogue

Along with the geographical and governmental changes in the San Ramon Valley have come some personal changes for the author since my last book was released November 11, 1977.

I lost my mother and my husband within two months of each other in 1980. My mother, Bertha Morris Boggini, had suffered a stroke March 5, 1974, and had resided in rest homes until she wore out October 23, 1980, three days after her eighty-second birthday, at Diablo Convalescent Hospital in Danville.

My husband, Alfred Bensen Jones, companion and helpmate for forty and one-half years, put up a valiant struggle against colon cancer following an operation July 18, 1978, at Kaiser Foundation Hospital in Walnut Creek. He continued his real estate business and his community and county involvements up to the very end. When the cancer overtook him, he slipped away December 20, 1980. He had turned sixty-seven years old on his final birthday October 24, 1980.

We had lived together in our Alamo home that we had built together with "love, sweat and tears," for thirty-two years. So in writing this book, *Be It Ever So Humble . . .*, I've not had their participation of enthusiasm and encouragement as in the past, and I've missed that. However, I have felt the great need to do this book so we will all have a record of these old homes and buildings, should they too some day meet their fate!

Once again, I will use my former newspaper column sign-off—OK? 'til next time?

Virgie V. Jones
August 1983

90

Index

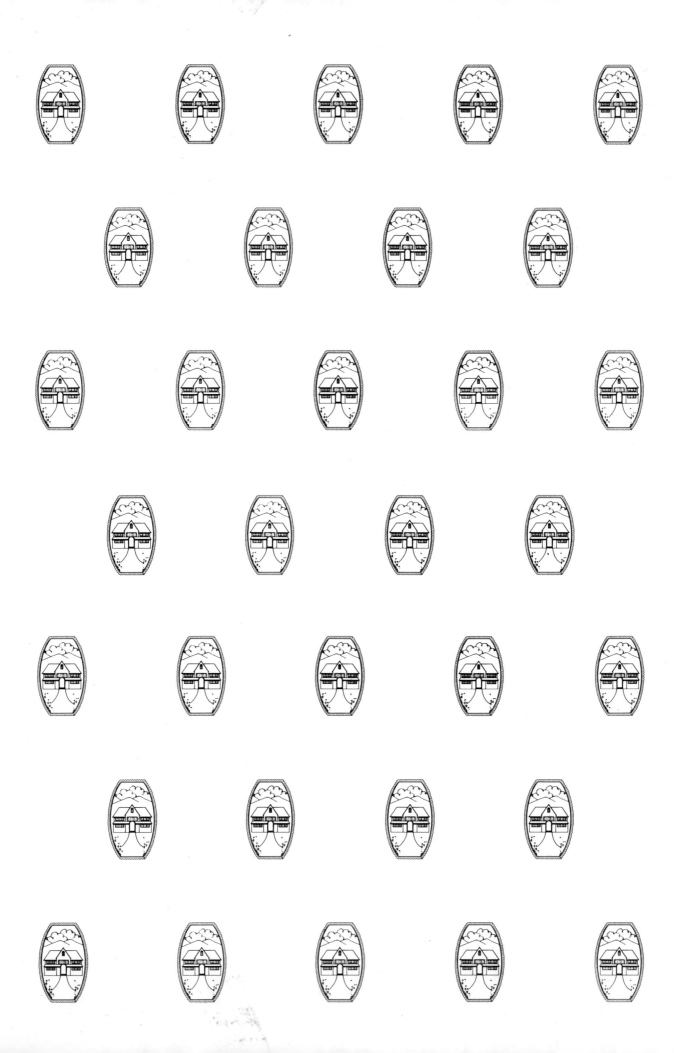